How to Hitch a Ride With No Thumbs:

Volume V of
The Travels of
Senator & Wendy V

- © 2013 by Wendy V. All rights reserved. No part of this publication may be reproduced or transmitted in any form or by any means, electronic or mechanical, including photocopy, recording, or any information storage and retrieval system, without the prior written consent of the author and/or publisher.

- cover art © 2013 by Adam Molella.

ISBN: 978-0-99150-934-8

for Senator—

Of course I'll run with you...

Commando Cody: I still think this is no trip for a woman.

Joan: Now don't start *that* again. You'll be very glad to have someone along who can cook your meals.

Ted: I'll say we will! Don't give her any more arguments.

Commando Cody: Okay, I like to eat too.

~Radar Men From the Moon (1952)
Chapter 1- "Moon Rocket"

Table of Contents

Introduction	i
40 Miles per Gallon, on a Good Day	1
Pickled Podcasting	29
Taken for Granite	49
Piece of Cake	79
Afterword	99
Bonus Tale: *The Pewter Candlestick*	101

Author's Note

See Author's Note, *How to Read a Compass in the Dark*. (By now it's a classic, and practically required reading in nine out of ten school districts.)

Introduction

I think that part of what I love about traveling is the idea of moving forward. Physically and mentally, you cannot stand still for very long when on vacation. There is no stagnation. As I write this, I am amazed that another school year is quickly reaching its end. So far, I would have to say that this has been the best year of my career. I had an incredible blend of students whose curiosity and quirkiness allowed me to be myself and share the topics I love. They pushed me in a good direction as they made their own journey through their senior year.

It has been a wonderful year, and I am exceedingly grateful. Senator and I had more fun than ever, enjoying plenty of laughs and conversations along the way. Recording live shows kept us busy, too. In between the mundane tasks of trying to comprehend new state teaching standards and juggling changes in procedures and evaluations, I was exposed to some very innovative and challenging music, thanks to some very late nights in Chicago and Milwaukee. Spending the late hours of the night surrounded by creative music-- sometimes while in a dreamlike state-- added to my forward momentum, like extra engines joining a train.

Existing in the midst of so much figurative motion must have been what kept me sane during our almost year-long dry spell from traveling. [*Gasp!*] By the time spring arrived though, I was ready to apply that internal propulsion to the road. I actually start to feel jittery if I go too long without traveling. I'm told that I inherited this trait from my grandpa, Carlo. Just like him, when I'm returning from one trip, I'm usually planning the next one. I can't help it. Like the old song says, "You gotta' move."

~Wendy V
April 2012

Chapter 1
40 Miles per Gallon, on a Good Day: Early April 2012

I kicked my feet up on the coffee table in the living room, letting the travel brochures and notes fall to the floor. Senator was passing through the room on a two minute break from working in his studio. "Hi Baby," he said as he leaned down to kiss the top of my head, taking note of the music that I was playing on the stereo.* "I should be done soon. The second set's almost mixed... at least until I listen to it tomorrow morning and decide that I don't like it." We both smiled at his familiar routine.

"Do you realize that, between the store and the studio, you haven't had a day off in a few months?" I pointed out. It was true. At just under three years of recording various configurations of the Chicago experimental jazz scene, Senator's

---

* Rough recordings of 1920s Delta blues were the closest I could get to an appropriate soundtrack for the Civil War narrative I was reading. After 2,800 pages of Shelby Foote's three-volume masterpiece, I had heard just about every blind reverend who ever set his guitar gospel to the wax.

talents were earning him regular bookings, if not regular cash. Meanwhile, he did not dare cut his hours at the store, as Barnes & Noble was already on shaky ground, often making the national financial headlines with plans for 'redirection' and 'reorganization'.* Whatever that meant, it did not sound secure. 'Better get while the gettin's good' was our motto.

Still, a break was definitely needed. In January, I parked myself at the computer to explore spring break options, informing Senator that he would be joining me for a romantic five day adventure... with no jobs of any kind involved. "We'll see," he teased, "What if there's a great show to record that week?"

"Then you'll have to tell 'em to schedule it near Gettysburg or Niagara Falls!" I shot back, simultaneously revealing the planned destinations. It had been far too long since we had run away together. We had even missed our trek to Door County the previous July. Too many projects had come up at once, and at that time, four days off could not be spared for nonproductive activities. In October, we had managed to squeeze in two nights of camping beyond the Cheddar Curtain, but now we were due to really get away.

While this trip was not associated with any pre-vacation disasters (thankfully), something interesting did occur. While scrolling around the internet, Senator learned that a band-- whose first two albums he had recorded-- would be touring North America in April. He was sure they would want him to record a show from the upcoming tour, but the Chicago date fell during the time we would be gone. There was no changing our plans, because it was the only week I could get off work, and reservations had already been made. Conveniently, however, the

---

* I have learned that any time a corporation starts throwing around words with the prefix 're', you can bet that the results will include more work and/or less pay.

band would be in Buffalo, New York, just a half hour's drive from Niagara Falls, where we would be that same morning. On top of that, they would be playing on the only possible night we could spare in our agenda. What could I say? It was too perfectly aligned to be an ignored coincidence. So, under strict family-meeting-proclaimed terms that it not be the sole focus of the trip, we added it to the schedule.

I counted down the weeks-- each one speeding by faster than the one before-- until we were at the end of March. The plan was to leave early on a Saturday morning, 6:00am to be precise. The early departure would allow us just enough hours to make it to our first stop, the Flight 93 Memorial, before it closed. As it turned out, we would be there on the last day of their winter hours, which meant that if we weren't through the gate by 4:00pm, we would be out of luck.

Finally our trip was only days away. Senator brought up the subject at dinner. "I've been thinking, and I don't know if you would want to do this, but what if we left Friday night instead?"

"YES!" I didn't hesitate to answer. "I wanted to suggest it, but I thought you'd be too rushed after work. And I was trying to save us a night's hotel expense."

Here Senator spoke words to live by (at least if you happen to be an overly frugal gal who, nevertheless, loves to travel). "Vacation is not the time to save money." *Amen, my true friend.* It was settled. Not only would we be less rushed, but we would also have the wonderful sensation of escaping together in the night, leaving teaching and retail and mixing and editing and housework and yard work behind.

When Friday came, I rushed home after work to take care of last minute preparations. An hour and a half later Senator was home, quickly packing the car with the necessary recording gear. I checked my bag for the essentials, grabbed some water for the road, and locked up the house. We were off, and heading east.

Traveling in any direction generally makes me happy, but

when you live in the Midwest, you must sacrifice the first several hours of your trip to bland, predictable scenery*. If you happen to be traveling east along Interstate 80, you also get to pay a hefty sum for this viewing privilege. Whereas Illinois prefers to hide its tolls among the thousands of dollars per year you pay in taxes for-- well, nobody actually knows for what-- other states have a more transparent system. You ride their interstates as long as desired, and pay your bill upon exiting.

When we crossed into Indiana we lined up to take our ticket from the attendant on duty. *What a simple yet unsatisfying job she had* I thought. Senator zipped us through the state in a few hours. As I said, it was nothing special to look at, even in the bask of twilight and moonlight, but it was wonderful to have uninterrupted hours just to talk as friends.

Soon we were at the state border, and the Indiana sign was thanking us for using their toll system. We pulled up to the booth, and I tried to interpret the ticket we had picked up on the west side of the state. It looked like the total would be seven-something. Or maybe eleven dollars. Who knew?

The booth was automated, and it instructed us to feed it our ticket. Senator tried, with no success. He tried again, this time while attempting to pay by credit card. Still no luck. I could feel the glares of the people in line behind us. I noticed that the digital sign read "EZ pass accepted". "I think it thinks we have an EZ pass," I ventured, realizing that I had just used the term "it thinks". "It's saying that we already paid." Senator shrugged, and pulled out the piece of paper that the machine had generated. He put the car into gear and accelerated as I tried to decipher the paper. It was a receipt, billed to someone else's credit card, saying that everything was paid. Hhmmm. Convenient, but still suspicious. I tucked the receipt into my purse for safekeeping. Part of me assumed we would need it

---

* I use the term loosely.

later for evidence when Indiana sent us a ticket for defying their toll road. Perhaps the most ironic part of the experience was the fact that there was a human employed to hand out tickets (which was the easy part), but a *machine* entrusted to determine amounts owed, accept methods of payment, and produce accurate receipts. Brilliant.

We then proceeded into Ohio, accepting the corresponding ticket for their turnpike. It had been a long day, and I was amazed that neither of us was tired. We agreed to drive another hour before stopping, which would put us at about midnight. Somewhere outside of not-so-holy Toledo, we found a clean, comfortable, reasonably priced hotel. Fifteen minutes after checking in, we were well into a deep sleep.

*   *   *

Saturday morning we did not sleep very late, which allowed us time to nibble some hotel breakfast. There was an ample but casual buffet set up, with plenty of dining room seating. I spied a small table in a far corner that we could claim once we had chosen our food. Senator loaded a plate with some eggs and toast. I decided to stick with fruit.

As I took the heavy ladle to scoop out a serving of fruit salad, my klutziness emerged, knocking it into a lid, which tipped off and started to fall, bringing a pitcher with it. Senator's fast reflexes saved the large, clangy lid from landing on the floor. His response also spared numerous patrons from dodging hunks of flying fruit. I breathed a sigh of relief. Various breakfast accoutrements being in their rightful places once again, we carried our plates to our table and calmly enjoyed the rest of the meal together.

After driving the remainder of Ohio ("thank you for using *our* turnpike"), we made our way southeast into Pennsylvania, and onto yet another turnpike. Our first official stop was the Flight 93 Memorial. While tourists regularly pay tribute to the site of the former Twin Towers and the Pentagon, few have made the pilgrimage to the quiet field in southern Pennsylvania, where dozens of people were murdered by Islamic extremists.

On September 11, 2001, forty people (crew and passengers) boarded a routine flight from Newark to San Francisco. When the plane altered its course to head back east, several of those on board surmised what had happened and overtook the plane, sending it hurling into open farmland, about 2½ hours west of Gettysburg. Of course no one survived, but it was later learned that the plane was bound for Washington, D.C.. Whether the target involved government officials, or even the White House is unclear, but it is safe to say that hundreds of lives were spared because of some very brave everyday heroes.

As expected, visiting the memorial was a quiet, solemn experience. Since it is not located within a town, there is about a four mile drive from the main road to the parking lot. It winds through mostly flat land, with some very gradual hills. Much of the ground is prairie grass or wildflowers, with clumps of trees scattered around. Upon reaching the parking lot, facilities are limited. A sign reminds you to pack out your garbage, as no trash cans are provided on the premises. The bathrooms, as I soon found out, are merely glorified outhouses.

We parked the car and grabbed the camera. For its sparseness, it was obvious that the memorial was well maintained. Senator and I joined hands and walked to the cement plaza that held five or six kiosks retelling the Flight 93 story. Though not personally touched by the tragedies of that day, it still raised our emotions to read the description of the events that led to innocent lives lost in a Pennsylvania field. As we read about the terrorists and remembered their celebrations on that day, it made our blood boil to think of the arrogant and perverse nature of such evil beings.

I had to skip the next kiosk. In permanent tribute to the individuals aboard the plane, a full color, enlarged photograph of each of their smiling faces filled one side. I am the girl who is incapable of crying in sappy movies, and who is completely unmoved by photos of cute puppies and babies, but it took some effort to swallow the lump in my throat and to hold the tears at bay. I only allowed myself a glimpse before moving on to the final panel, which offered some resolution by focusing on the pride we Americans can take in our heritage of courage and justice.*

Beyond the kiosks, a small outdoor amphitheatre with rows of cement benches arranged in a semi-circle faces a flag pole. There is no formal visitor center, but a short walk along a paved path leads to the wall of honor. Each panel of the wall is engraved with the name of one passenger or crew member aboard the flight. From a distance, one can see the actual site of the crash, marked only with a large rock and some flowers. Walking out to the site from the wall of honor, however, is strictly limited to family members of victims. Only a small sign enforces this, but everyone seems to respect the reasonable request.

The Flight 93 Memorial is not an all-day event. In fact, we toured it in about thirty minutes. I was still very glad to have gone, though. I felt it was my duty as a United States citizen who was capable of making the pilgrimage. It cannot be described as 'fun', but it is significant, and its impact still resonates with me.

*   *   *

The drive to Bedford was less than two hours long, allowing us to check into our hotel a little earlier than planned. We thought we might have time for a swim, but a small pool filled with a large brood of kids was enough to send us back up

---

* I pray that this is not a decaying trait of my country. Given the state of society today, my realist nature has a hard time picturing current and future generations putting down their iPads and video games, or turning off their reality shows to answer the call of duty. I hope I am wrong...

to our room. We could always try again after dinner. Apparently skipping the swim was the right choice, since we both fell asleep soon after lying down.

When we awoke, it was dinner time. Ah, dinner. Or, more accurately, ah choice of dining establishment. Though we pack multiple activities into trip agendas, we generally do not make a point of where we eat. While planning this trip however, I stumbled upon information about Jean Bonnet Tavern. Immediately I made reservations. Why the sudden enthusiasm about dining out? It may have had something to do with the fact that this stone tavern has been in existence since the 1760s, welcoming hungry and weary travelers to its massive timbered dining room.

It also didn't hurt that the room was filled with candlelight, the atmosphere was warm, and the crowd was jovial.* Our host showed us to our table, and we took our seats in the classic colonial spoke-backed wooden chairs. The pewter dishes completed the scene, but having only nibbled fruit and nuts during the day, we were ready for those dishes to be filled.

Mixed vegetable tempura appetizer? Yes please. Portobello mushroom sandwich on homemade roll? I believe I

---

* We were both inspired by the setting. Senator suggested that I write a short story about it. The fact that I had not written any fiction since high school, and what I had written had long ago been destroyed (with no regret) did not seem to faze him. He supplied the last line of the story, and I was assigned to "do the rest". I dismissed the idea verbally, but toyed with it in my mind throughout the rest of the trip. About two weeks after we returned, I decided to give it a shot. With a half used notebook and a pen, I sat down at the kitchen table to jot down a few ideas, and maybe write a few paragraphs. Two and a half hours later I set my pen down and stood up to stretch. *The Pewter Candlestick* had virtually written itself. Later that night I read it to him, by candlelight of course.

will, thank you. Sip of the signature house ale, Liberty Pole Pilsner? Why not? We tried to eat slowly, but I think our server was surprised at our empty dishes when she came to check on us.

"Room for dessert?..." she offered, sliding a tray of samples in front of us. Naturally. Being vegetarians, we had to forgo the herb roasted pork loin and the lobster ravioli, but now we could indulge in something more suited to traditional early American fare.

"We'll try a piece of the oatmeal pie [*A delicious, mild flavored dessert that will exceed your expectations*], and a piece of the pecan pie [*Loaded with pecans and flavored with honey and bourbon*]," Senator announced. As we waited for our sweet delights to arrive, Senator reminded me of a horror movie we both love, starring Boris Karloff. *The Body Snatcher* pits Karloff in yet another diabolic role, set in a colonial era tavern like Jean Bonnet. For good measure, Bela Lugosi rounds out the cast.* Without giving away any dark surprises, I will only tell you that the name "Toddy" was added to many of our sentences the rest of the evening.

Satiated beyond what any colonial probably ever experienced, we concluded our feast and drove back to the hotel. Bedford, Pennsylvania, is a small town that has bridged the delicate gap of respecting its history while offering ample modern amenities. In the bustling downtown, many businesses set up shop in old stone buildings, and 200-year old farmhouses still dot the outlying areas. Large stone, wooden beams, and mortar stand firm as a testament to the materials of an earlier form of construction. Adding to the effect, homes all over

---

* If you don't know who these actors are, immediately buy a classic horror film collection of each, call in sick from your job, close all of the curtains in the house, light a few candles, and enjoy... Yes, Toddy!

Bedford greet twilight by lighting single electric candles in windows that face the streets. It's a simple practice that at some point must have caught on all around town. By nightfall, the area is peppered with a mysterious twinkle.

It had been a long day, but we still had plans to swim. These plans again were postponed when we learned that the same family was still taking residence in the pool. "I guess we'll try in the morning," I said. *Unless they're sleeping there...* Crummy cable reruns it is.

Sunday morning we woke up to the sounds of The Family outside our door in the hallway. They were noisy, but at least they were leaving. *The pool was ours!* We put on our swimwear and lightly jogged down the two flights of stairs and around the corner to the pool.

Finally, it was empty. The water rippled slightly, showing no sign of the boisterous clan that had previously held it captive. Off to the side, we found a dry spot for our towels. Slowly we edged our way into the water. The icy water. I gasped and Senator hunched his shoulders up. Wow! He was eventually able to immerse his whole body, briefly, but I just couldn't do it. I was freezing. So much for that.

There was the consolation prize of the jacuzzi, however. Senator set the timer on the wall, and we lowered ourselves into the bubbles. It felt good. I still needed to exercise, but for the moment I just sat and relaxed. The tub faced a steeply sloping hill which contained the town's largest cemetery, a view which I found both amusing and pleasing. I closed my eyes for just a moment.

Before I got too comfortable, I decided that I had better perform some version of a workout. Remembering the indulgence of the previous night's meal, I developed a generic routine of kicks, tricep dips, and arm paddles. Though the movement was fluid and the water eased some of the burden of the weight, I still managed to work up quite a sweat. Senator got out and dried off. This gave me more room to push the workout a little harder. "Hey, let me know when it says 8:25. Then I'll have my half hour in." Senator glanced at the clock. Twelve minutes remained. I was getting tired, but I was committed.

"Okay, time's up," Senator called. I let my legs drop to their natural vertical position and eased myself over to the stairs. The cool air felt good as I stepped out of the water. I had expected that strange, heavy feeling one gets when exiting a whirlpool, but I did not expect the sensation that was immediately sweeping over me. I was instantly weak and shaky to the point of needing help just to get to a chair.

Then the nausea set in. *Oh, God, no. Please don't let me puke. Not here anyway.* My mind was clear, but I was so exhausted that I could barely form words.

At the same time, I realized that I had to say something. Senator was getting concerned. "I'm... um..." I squeaked out. I couldn't remember the last time I had felt such complete loss of strength. I was not exactly sure what was going to happen, but things were not moving in a direction that I liked.

The outside frame of my vision was growing very dark, as though a camera's lens was constricting. I could only see a foggy picture in the center. Then I began to lose my hearing. Sound seemed like it was moving farther away, all the while garbled as if underwater.

More than anything, though, I just wanted a drink of water. I was so thirsty. For a second I thought of the Civil War book I had been reading. *Why did soldiers always want a drink of water when they were dying?* I didn't want to scare Senator any more than I already had, so I tried to let him know that I was okay, but fading fast. "I... might... faint... It's okay..." I quietly announced, hating the fact that I probably sounded like a drama queen with a woefully limited vocabulary.

I wondered if I would be unconscious for a long time. That would be horrible. I tried to keep talking to Senator. I knew that I was putting him in a bad position. It's always easier to be the patient than the worrying caregiver. I kept telling myself that I had to stay alert. My internal monologue went something like this:

Alright, now this is just plain stupid. You worked out-- hard. Goody for you. Now look what you've done. You look ridiculous, and you are scaring a perfectly sweet guy who just wanted to have a nice sit in the whirlpool with you. And think about this: if you go unconscious, there is the distinct possibility that you will miss going to Gettysburg this afternoon. Gettysburg! You've been looking forward to this for months. WAKE UP! WAKE UP! And don't even think about throwing up. As soon as you do, some kid will come in to use the pool and run out screaming, drawing leagues of unwanted attention. Listen to the sounds around you. Senator's talking. The water is flopping against the filter door. Look up. See Senator. See the pool. See the man in the exercise room, whose back is to the window, and who has missed this entire spectacle. See the cemetery. Wait-- scratch that last part. Look back at Senator. Stay awake!

And that, I believe, is how I actually willed myself from going unconscious. I emerged from the limbo as quickly as I had slipped into it. When sound fully returned, I knew I had won. The nausea passed, and I felt like I was breathing fresh, clean air again. A moment later my strength started to return. The entire event only lasted ten or fifteen minutes, but it seemed like I had been in that chair for hours.

Physically, I would be fine. Mentally, I felt like an idiot. "I swear I didn't fake that!" I blurted out. Not that I make a habit of such performances; I just didn't know what else to say.

"Yeah, I know," Senator said quietly as he elevated my feet. "You looked gray."

"Gray? The color gray?" I was simultaneously disgusted and intrigued. I wish I could have seen it. Or maybe I don't. Senator now deemed me stable enough for him to leave for a few seconds to get me water and a cold cloth for my head. I thought about the time in Utah that he had to hand-feed me oranges after an apple cleanse gone horribly wrong in the 100°F+ degree heat. We are both in what doctors label "excellent health", so how do I get myself into these dumb situations?

The crisis was over, so we carefully walked the stairs back to our room. My strength and my color had completely returned. I actually felt rejuvenated in a weird sort of way. In less than an hour, we were packed and checking out. With coffee in tow, we were on our way to Gettysburg.

*   *   *

The drive from Bedford was just as lovely as the town itself. We wound our way through rocky hills and valleys. Farms dotted the countryside, many of which were composed of stones taken from the ground. Nineteenth century brick homes were also well represented and well preserved. This part of Pennsylvania is tidily tucked into the Allegheny Mountains, and time and technology have not spoiled its landscape. This makes it all the more appropriate as a gateway to the Pennsylvania Dutch Country further east.

Just before noon, the neat and narrow streets of Gettysburg were in view. We approached from the west, but one can enter Gettysburg from any of about ten roads that converge there. Having so many routes allowed for the strategic movement of several thousand troops in that hot July of 1863. That is one of the reasons that the battle occurred where it did.

Gettysburg is well marked and very clean. It is easy for the tourist to make his or her way through the streets, provided he or she is not in a hurry. Though an international landmark, the town's population is still only 8,000 or so. There are no interstates there. Driving slowly is hardly a drawback, though. It allows plenty of time to gaze at the buildings. The concentration of Civil War era homes and businesses that are still in daily use is staggering. On both sides of all of the main roads, brick and wooden structures continue to serve as inns, taverns, bookshops, restaurants, and other, more modern establishments.

Crossing through the downtown area led us to the visitor center. A lot had changed since I had last visited as a sixteen-year old. The beautiful expanded structure sat among three or four parking lots, and a cement walk led to a statue of Lincoln, seated on a bench. Unlike some of the other tourists, we were not tempted to take our photo with Old Abe. After all, we could see him standing in our local park, debating Stephen Douglas, anytime we wanted.

Once inside, our first stop was the expected introductory film, narrated by the expected Morgan Freeman. He explained how the two armies met, how the fighting was intense, and how a late night conference extended it to a third bloody day. In addition to contemplating the war, I thought about how appropriate it was that a documentary on Gettysburg was hosted by a black man whose last name is Freeman. Think about it.

Upon exiting the theatre, we moved upstairs to the cyclorama. If you are like me, the suffix '-orama' immediately conjures up some sort of entertainment venue from 1956. Inside the imagined place, there are fat men smoking cigars and highly coiffed women daring to wear slacks in public. On the walls are smiling cartoon people holding martini glasses. The ceiling is covered with sparse, geometric starbursts, made out of some sort of foam that has since been ruled too toxic for human interaction.

The Gettysburg cyclorama forever shattered this image for me. I learned that the term 'cyclorama' was actually used in the late 1800s, when the painting was created, to describe its 360° vista. A Frenchman named Paul Philippoteaux painted the enormous Pickett's Charge battlefield scene to honor its heroes and fallen. At 359' long, and 27' high, the incredible attention to detail and acute reproduction of a sense of movement place the viewer in the midst of the action. Add to that the museum's lighting effects and surround sound recording, and you have a multimedia experience to rival anything the 21st Century has yet to produce. I swear I could almost smell the smoke...

The rest of the museum contained hundreds of thousands of bits of memorabilia from the War Between the States. Journals, uniforms, half-destroyed battle flags, and even musical instruments each told of their role in the drama. A drummer boy's drum that had sat silent for the past 150 years seemed ready to beat out orders and formations at a moment's notice. Of course, civilians' perspectives were recognized, too. Most notably was poor Jennie Wade. The local young lady was working in her home when a musket ball crashed through her house, killing her instantly, and forever memorializing her as the only civilian killed at Gettysburg.

Armed with our own arsenal of far more facts than we could ever hope to remember, we set out for the highlight of the military park-- the battlefield itself. Naturally, we broke the chief rule of historical touring[*], but we still made it through the entire drive. The 28-mile loop wove in and out of the west side of town, encompassing sixteen stops and countless memorials that defined where each army stood at various times during the three-day clash. One of my favorites was the emotional Louisiana memorial. It depicted a herald angel swooping over a fallen soldier, suggesting peace and hope among tragedy.

Appropriately, the driving tour ended at the Soldiers' National Cemetery. On grassy spans, under oak and pine trees, Union and Confederate soldiers-- most identified by only a number-- lay side by side, each convinced of their righteousness in the fight to preserve freedom. We walked along the rows of anonymous graves for a while, passing a guide who was retelling one of the familiar stories to a tour group. It seemed like fiction, but there, as thousands of souls can attest, it was all too real.

The Gettysburg battlefield was beautiful and wild and solemn and draining. Yes, all of those. By the time we were

---

[*]not allowing enough time to properly observe each point of interest

finished driving it, we were ready to check into our accommodations for a quick rest. Just two miles down the road, the Lightner House added one more dimension to the battle.

In 1861, the home's owner built his brick home on several acres of farmland. He was happy to retire to the peace and comfort of country living outside a small town. Just two years later, however, he found himself unintentionally drawn into the fray. With so many wounded in the three days of fighting at Gettysburg, Mr. Lightner's parlors were quickly commandeered as hospital rooms. Kitchen and dining room tables were conscripted as operating tables for the surgeons and their bone saws. Just behind one of those parlors was our room.

Though we strained our ears, no ghosts from either army cried out. In fact, the only groaning we heard was our stomachs. We settled in for a few minutes, then left again to drive back into town. It had started to drizzle, making warm food even more inviting.

In retrospect, it would have made sense to find somewhere Civil War-y to eat. Better yet, we could have gone truly authentic by renouncing our vegetarianism in favor of half-rotten salt pork and stale hardtack. Ever on the lookout for ethnic food we cannot get at home, however, we opted for a Thai restaurant.

Outside, the rain picked up speed while we feasted on rice with carrots, mushrooms, peppers, onions, and those adorable little ears of baby corn. I believe there was basil and ginger involved, but beyond that, I am a consistent failure when it comes to reproducing great Thai dishes. Our server must have sensed this, because she did not even bother to offer us chopsticks. They only would have slowed us down anyway.

After dinner we drove around town for a little while before stopping in front of an ice cream shop. Gastronomically speaking, ice cream does not usually follow Thai food, but we were sucked in by the fact that it was homemade ice cream, produced and served in yet another beautiful Victorian brick building. As we waited in line for our mint chocolate chip and cookies n' cream (not combined), I studied the interior of the building and read the plaque on the wall. During the war, a student from the nearby seminary ran into the home to seek shelter when the cannon and bullets started to fly. He wrote that the Confederates took all of the food, leaving only a small scrap of beef and some coffee.

It was hard to imagine firepower ripping through the town; we were sitting in such a casual atmosphere, enjoying our dessert and sampling each other's flavors. The rain continued to pour down the window. I guess if we had really wanted to connect with the battle scene, we could have forked over some cash and signed up for a ghost tour with the poor souls manning their ticket table out in the rain. While the dampness may have added to the ambiance, no one was signing up for a walking tour on such a dreary night. As we finished our last bits of ice cream, we saw the drenched men pack up their table and leave.

We did not join any tours, but we did take advantage of the late closing time of the battlefield. Unlike most national or state parks, the Gettysburg battlefield is open until 10:00pm. Though we had already driven the loop earlier that day, rain, clouds, darkness, and a low rolling fog presented an irresistible combination. Again we turned down the narrow side street that led us to the marked road.

Though it was only blocks away from the downtown, the lack of any street lights made it seem as if we had gone miles away from civilization. Each stop was well marked, but the overcast purple-gray sky made it hard to navigate. Twists and turns that were obvious in the daylight now required careful attention. At certain angles, only the shadowy silhouettes of giant monuments were visible, and only once did we pass another car. If you are fortunate enough to be in Gettysburg on a cold spring night, when mist and fog blur the lines of the road and reality, this is the way to see the battlefield. Though I cannot report that we encountered anything of the paranormal sort, there was a striking solemnity in our nighttime tour.

*   *   *

Monday morning found us starting our day at a two-person table in the Lightner House parlor. I do believe it was the only time we had ever eaten in a room that had served as a makeshift army hospital. Hhmmm. It was a bit odd to think that some young man could have had his leg sawed off in the very spot where my egg and cheese strata now sat. I suddenly felt like I could use some brandy...

As we enjoyed the view of the home's gardens, we could overhear a British family at the next table. Accuse me of stereotyping, but the British simply have better manners than Americans.[*] Two parents and their two extremely well-behaved children (ages eight and eleven, maybe) were eating and discussing the day's plans to see the battlefield. The older child, a girl, was interested in the history of the house, and she asked many questions as her eyes darted around the antiques in the room. The mother, concerned that her daughter was behaving inappropriately in public, mildly reprimanded her. "Dah-leeng, *please* try to focus on your day ahead! Stop looking around the room..."

"But I thought that was what we were here fo'," came the logical and precocious answer. Touché! She was my kind of girl. I have always said that I can teach any student who is curious. When it comes to the quest for knowledge, social niceties be damned!

We finished our meal and went back to our room. We had just enough time for a short walk around the grounds. The sun was shining, but it was still chilly. I flipped up the hood on

---

[*] with the possible exception of the Sex Pistols, although I've never breakfasted near them, so I can't say for sure

my sweater and pulled in closer to Senator as we hiked. "Where's your jacket?!" he demanded. Where was that eleven year old? I could have used a snappy retort. In less than fifteen minutes we had trekked through the mud down into the forest, across the field, through the gardens and back again. With our brief walk complete, it was time to leave Gettysburg and head north.

The drive up Route 15 took us through central Pennsylvania toward New York. For the most part the ride was uneventful, taking us along a scenic river and over a few low-slung hills. The only part that sticks out in my mind is the section of weird signs that we encountered. About an hour and a half into our journey, in a nondistinct area dotted with a few small towns, we saw a road sign advising us to "Beware aggressive drivers". I looked at the people in the next lane. The middle-aged couple did not seem particularly threatening, so we dismissed the warning.

A few miles later we saw another sign. This one reminded us to "Stay alert!" We were both wide awake, so no problem there. Not long after that sign we were made privy to another piece of the puzzle. "High DUI area" was hardly a stirring invitation to visit their fair city. How bad of a problem does a town have to have for it to install permanent signs about the incapability of its drivers? To complicate matters further, the other side of the road had a yellow sign depicting the universal image of an Amish buggy. So let's review. We've got pissed off drunk drivers who may or may not be driving vehicles manufactured during any portion of the last 200 years. A final sign suggested that we "Buckle up... next million miles". Good advice. Maybe we actually do have a friend in Pennsylvania.

By late afternoon we arrived in Niagara Falls. I had visited twice before, once as a teenager on my last family vacation, and once with friends. I recall both times being somewhat rushed, with just a few hours to spend in the park.

This time, however, I was here on an overnight date, complete with a romantic inn just a two minute walk from the thundering waters.

I began to question the romantic reputation of the city, however, as we reached its outskirts. We bounced and jerked our way down the road that led to the heart of the town, avoiding potholes whenever possible, (which was not often). Until the last few blocks of the drive, ugly factories and run-down homes lined the crumbling street. I did not remember this part. Perhaps I had come from another direction.

Our hotel was positioned on the last main street before a bridge transformed the land into Canada. It was elegant and quiet, tastefully decorated in an English Tudor style, although I'm not sure what that had to do with northwestern New York. Just a block behind our hotel, however, the town changed drastically. In short, it looked like a ghetto dump. Half of the storefronts were boarded up in response to failed businesses or vandals or both. Garbage littered the streets in some spots, and seedy people milled around with no good purpose.

A few such people almost had a hand in making our vacation take a very bad turn. We were on a quest for interesting food, so we were excited to see three different Indian restaurants listed in the phone book. We did not realize that they were so close to our inn, so we took the car. We parked on the street and went to check out the first one. Only one man was in the restaurant, which looked more like a take-out joint. Food was being prepared, and the hours were posted, but he curtly informed us that they were "closed for the day". It was only 4:30pm, but the look on his face did not leave any room for argument.

Strike one. We drove a little further to Indian restaurant #2. Again we parked and got out to assess the situation. We were only gone for a minute or two before we learned that this establishment had long ago gone out of business. This turned out to be a blessing. In the brief time we were away from our car, a woman and a younger girl (mother/daughter team?) had pulled up right behind our car and were scoping out its contents from the sidewalk. Senator noticed that as soon as we started walking across the street to our car, they quickly turned away, lamely pretending to window shop in the closest storefront. I say "lamely" because it too was boarded up.

What was the deal with this place? What about the natural rugged beauty of the falls? What about the quaint traditional honeymoon destination of millions of mid-century Americans? What about the tourists coming in from Canada? Was this what we were offering as a first impression of the greatest country on Earth? Frankly, the city of Niagara Falls is an embarrassment.

As it turned out, Indian restaurant #3, though completely unoccupied by other diners, was open. We were greeted by a very friendly man about my age, who tripled as host, server, and cashier. We relaxed a little as we sampled delicious spicy curries and naan. "Family meeting," announced Senator. I could see where this was going. "I know you don't want me to drag all of the recording gear into our room, but there is no way in the world we are leaving that stuff in the car overnight." His voice indicated the period at the end of the sentence.

Up to this point I had been adamant about keeping the overall logistics of a vacation/recording gig as simple as possible. I hated the thought of him lugging heavy equipment through our hotel, especially since there was no elevator. I also did not want to look like the Beverly Hillbillies, but in this case, I couldn't really argue. Smashed windows and police reports would have certainly put a damper on the trip. After dinner, unloading the car was the first objective.

With the gear safely stowed in our room, and our car parked for the night with a prayer, we walked over to the American side of the falls. We looked out over the top of the spray. Not much more than a glorified handrail separated us from the millions of gallons of water rushing over the rocky cliff. The utter power of the water was staggering.

Another fifty yards led us to the Rainbow Bridge, pedestrian gateway to Ontario, Canada. I double-checked that our passports were secure in my bag. I did not want to have to explain to a border patrol guard that our identity documents had blown away over the windy bridge. What then? We would be stuck midway, suspended over international waters, nomads unclaimed by either country. All such catastrophes avoided, we entered Canada without a hitch.

The walk along the Canadian side of the falls further emphasized the glaring differences in each country's approach to the attraction. Though the sun was setting, we never for a moment felt unsafe. Families, couples, and other tourists walked the long stretch, taking in the superior views of the Canadian falls. Further up the hill, the savvy town had turned several blocks into a hopping entertainment destination. Funhouses, restaurants, shops, gamerooms, clubs, and more drew a steady stream of visitors, even on a Monday night. By contrast, the American side had one crummy, half-empty tee shirt shop. For the privilege of buying an overpriced piece of junk there, you would also have to navigate through the ongoing building construction. Oh, Canada!

The night air was chilly, enhanced by a steady breeze coming off of the water. Senator put his arms around me as we watched the colored lights illuminate the falls. White changed to green, yellow, red, and other colors. Twice a bat flew up in front of us. When we had viewed the entire aquatic rainbow, it was time to walk back to the mother country.

The wind blew harder, and the walk seemed longer on the way back, possibly because my shoes had begun to pinch my feet approximately two hours earlier. Entering the United States is not as casual of an experience as entering Canada. It is also not as cheap. To Canada= free. To United States= 50¢ apiece. And you had better have cash. After paying the fee, we waited in a cold, boxlike metal room, severely instructed not to enter the customs room until called.

The guard motioned for me to enter, so I did. I presented my passport and driver's license dutifully. The guy gave me a strange look. "Isn't he with you?" he asked, indicating Senator, whom I had left back in The Box.

"Oh, yes!" I answered. "I didn't know if I could bring him with. I mean..." *Oh, never mind what I meant.* I was happy when he passed us both along undetained. I was even happier when I kicked off my shoes and concluded the cold night in a warm bubble bath.

*   *   *

We slept well, partly due to the knowledge that nothing of real value had been left in the car, and partly due to the fact that we may have been the only ones staying at the inn that night. Both the hallways and the downstairs restaurant were elegant but empty. We certainly did not have any trouble getting a window seat at breakfast. For some reason though, the service was incredibly slow.

While we waited for our food, we chatted and looked at the magnificent view of the falls. It was a crisp and clear morning-- the kind that invigorates the soul and motivates one for the day's events. It was fortunate that our moods were bright, as the food was not contributing to the bliss. Apparently it is possible for one to order "the skillet" (served in a cast iron pan), and not receive a hot meal. Piled in a small cold pan were raw vegetables, shredded-but-nowhere-near-melted cheese, and some desperately-trying-to-be-warm eggs. We stared at it for a moment before picking through the pieces. "At least no one can accuse them of using a microwave," I mused.

Breakfast, needless to say, was over quickly. We loaded the car and drove the block to our first stop of the day. It wasn't that we had become too lazy to walk such a short distance; the visitor center offered the distinct benefit of a gated lot. It was worth the few bucks it cost to park there just to know our gear wouldn't be stolen.

We had, of course, viewed the falls for several hours the night before, but I wanted to get the factual history and background information to round out the experience. Thus, into the visitor center we went. The scene inside was typical of what we had seen around town on the American side. Much of the building was vacant, and no one looked particularly happy to be there.

This was evident when we tried to buy tickets for an IMAX movie about the falls' origins. Just ten minutes before showtime, the box office looked deserted. Other tourists looked around in confusion, too. Finally a very flustered and frustrated woman opened a curtain (think Great and Powerful Oz), and took our money while muttering something about too few people trying to cover shifts.

Unfortunately, I cannot say that the movie made up for the poor quality of the visitor center. It was billed as a historical journey about human interaction with the falls, and it started to deliver on that promise for the first five minutes or so. It opened with a Native American legend, but quickly degenerated into disjointed tales of sensationalism surrounding the falls.[*] Somehow a fairly realistic reenactment of French fur traders morphed into a crappy 1960s reenactment of the rescue of some stupid boaters, to whom it did not occur that fishing above a 183' drop might not be prudent.

In summary, there is absolutely no need to pay for any part of the Niagara Falls experience, save the parking. Definitely do that. Then get out and walk along the American falls. Stroll around Goat Island, which gives a unique view of the top of the

---

*   as if their natural splendor was not impressive enough

Canadian falls. Then take your passport and your money and go stimulate the Canadian economy across the bridge. You will enjoy a safe, clean, romantic view of one of this continent's natural wonders.

*   *   *

We kissed Niagara Falls good-bye and drove south to Buffalo, arriving in plenty of time to focus on the evening's work. Senator was booked to record a jazz trio in a venue that was housed in part of an old gothic church. We found the place easily, and he went inside to check out the logistics of the room. Fortunately, the curator permitted him to unload the gear, too. Perfect-- now we would have time for a much needed nap.

Just two miles down the road, we checked into our bed and breakfast and met Karen, the owner. Karen was a kindred spirit whose down-to-earth, bright attitude was infectious. She kept her sense of humor as she fumbled with new technology and told us about the house and her beloved town. Immediately she treated us like she was our fun aunt, pointing out treats and amenities to spoil us for a night.

Napping was first priority, but we still had a few hours to kill, so we decided to take in the Buffalo Historical Museum. The building reminded me of the 1890s Chicago architecture that dominated the landscape of the Magnificent Mile, a la the World's Columbian Exposition. Inside, the museum's featured exhibit centered around a painting of the Trial of Red Jacket. Red Jacket, whose name was somehow related to his ability to captivate an audience, was a Seneca tribe activist during the early years after the country won independence from Britain. He was a known peacemaker, as denoted by the silver medal given to him by none other than George Washington.

We browsed other exhibits as well. One told of a local female architect who held her own 100 years ago, even though she was only paid about 10% of what her male counterparts earned. Well ahead of her time, she encouraged other females in her profession to branch out to loftier projects, rather than simply focusing on homes. Another room highlighted a variety of items, united only in that they were all made in Buffalo. From clocks, to cereals, to electronic parts, all items reflected the region's pride. Contrary to the Niagara Falls visitor center, this museum was worth the time and money invested.

Before long it was time to head back to Hallwalls, the venue where we would record. It was exciting to be working somewhere different. At home, we record at a handful of places betweeen Chicago and Milwaukee, but we had never worked outside of the Midwest. The curator at Hallwalls was easygoing and very accommodating, which also helped.

We set up with plenty of time to spare and took our places in the rear of the room, computer lights flickering in anticipation. As we waited for the show to start, a college couple came in and sat right next to me. I was a little surprised because the room was nowhere near full, but I nodded an acknowledgment of their presence and turned back to Senator. Then the drunk, preppy college guy started telling me about his professor. It seemed that the teacher was entirely unreasonable in marking Preppy's paper late, just because it was... late. "He knew I had the flu," Preppy pointed out. I smiled weakly.

He rambled on some more, simultaneously making out with his date*, but I was not paying attention to him. I was more intrigued by her. She seemed normal and competent enough, yet she was with *him*. What was the appeal? He wasn't dumb and hot; he was dumb and dorky. Unattractive, if I may be completely truthful. Maybe his daddy had money.

Five minutes into the first set, the alcohol in his system won, and he passed out. During the intermission, they left. Thank goodness. Senator's theory-- and I am inclined to agree-- is that they came to the concert because someone told them that

---

* takes talent!

the music would be 'cutting edge', and therefore they must make an appearance to say they were there. I imagined them raving about it to all of their friends the next day, making up a name for the band, since they had no idea who had actually played.

Overall, the music was intense, the recording went well, and most importantly, we had fun. Senator even managed to squeeze a small workout in, hauling his gear up a long flight of stairs. (The curator later apologized for forgetting to tell us about an elevator located elsewhere in the building.) No harm done. It was a great night, and despite invitations to join the band for socializing afterward, we went straight back to our room. We were looking forward to a long, quiet soak... provided we didn't fall asleep during the two-mile commute.

*   *   *

Coffee, muffins, and fruit were set out for us the next morning, compliments of Karen. It was self-serve, with no fuss. I liked her style. A few minutes after we sat down, she popped in to join us. Before we knew it, we had pleasantly blown half an hour, discussing everything from art, to politics, to music, to the economy, to traveling, to real estate. She made me want to visit Buffalo again. Who knows? Maybe we will.

We packed the car and I arranged my assorted maps in the front seat. There was nothing left to do but head home. We had fit a lot into five days, but that was nothing new. Bringing equipment to do work while on vacation was. I was pleased that we had achieved a balance between work and play. Both were satisfying, and we agreed that we would do it again if the occasion arose.

The rest of the drive home was uneventful, until we were pulled over in western Indiana. Senator was behind the wheel, "keeping pace with traffic", as he would say. As a lifelong realist, I am convinced that, even if I was only going five miles over the limit, and everyone else was going fifteen miles over, I would be the one they targeted, especially if outside of Illinois. I shared this belief with Senator, but given my reputation for being overly cautious at times, it was graciously ignored.

He pulled to the side of the road while I fished out the license, insurance, and registration. The genuinely friendly police officer walked up to the window. "Hello, folks," she said, matter-of-factly. I passed the paperwork over and she went through a shortened version of the "Do-you-know-why-I-pulled-you-over?" speech. We expected her to write a speeding ticket, but instead she gave us a warning.

Then she went on to ask us several questions about our vehicle. These were not suspicious questions. She wanted to know about things like gas mileage ("40mpg on a good day") and our satisfaction with the car ("completely satisfied"). She even sheepishly asked if we would mind telling her what we paid for it, explaining that she and her husband were considering a new car purchase. Of course we obliged the woman who had just granted us mercy.

The experience was strange and humorous. I guess much of our life together falls into that category. Just like the unplanned adventures that occur while taking trips, it keeps it all interesting, and I would not trade any of it. Even so, I will always keep my registration and insurance papers in my glove box.

Chapter 2
Pickled Podcasting: Early July 2012

It boggles my mind that there are still people throughout this great land that labor under the delusion that Chicago equals constant cold. The occasional legendary blizzards of the past few decades have permanently etched images of sideways-blowing snow and cars buried beyond their windshields into the minds of non-Illinoisans, or even natives with extremely short-term memory. Forgotten each spring, as the remnants of dirty drifts melt into puddles to bathe the earliest buds, are the horrendous bouts of heat and humidity that transform the Midwest into an inland version of the Gulf Coast.

In March, the greater metropolitan area of Chicagoans congratulate themselves on surviving bitter winter wind chills, which can feel like -20°F. In April life is hopeful, and those far enough outside the radius of regular violent crime dare to open their windows to let in the cool night air for pleasant sleeping. May brings consistent warmth, but not without a few decidedly hot days. By early June, it all comes back into the memory. Oh yes. This is summer in Northern Illinois; prepare to sweat.

The meteorologists promised it would be a "hot one". I somehow doubted that that was a scientific term, but who was I to argue? On the other hand, maybe we would luck out. Last fall they had predicted a winter so harsh that it would send lifelong Chicago residents fleeing to the South. What proceeded to materialize was the mildest winter of my entire lifetime. Perhaps this dire prediction of weeks in the 90s and 100s would fizzle out into a balmy, breezy streak of 78°F days.

No such luck. Record high after record high was broken from one coast to the other before we had even reached the halfway point of the season. Despite my lifelong distaste for summer weather, two factors worked in our favor. First, our home is air conditioned.[*] Second, because June turned out to be Senator's busiest month of recording so far, he was often confined to his cool basement studio.

Summer had opened in a blur of activity. We both continued to work, reserving five consecutive days in June to record a dozen jazz sets as part of a festival. As we dragged ourselves home on the last night, Senator reminded me that we were recording again the following Thursday. I think I just nodded. That was still four days away, and in the meantime, he had to dive into a new and very involved music project that had a deadline of July 1st.

One week after that gig, we were booked to record yet another concert. Though Senator continued to burn the candle at both ends-- and often in the middle-- things were coming along well. The music was great, and if he could wrap things up by the end of June, he could take a break from studio work, allowing us to travel in July. Sweetening the deal was the fact that my summer school class had ended that afternoon. I sat back in my seat as we drove into the city, feeling like we were shifting into a good groove.

Senator was feeling something, too. His groove, however, involved stomach cramping. He mentioned it briefly, placing

---

[*] I might not be writing this book now if it wasn't.

possible blame on a jicama he had eaten a few hours earlier, but he did not complain. By the time we arrived at the venue and started setting up, though, I could tell he was very uncomfortable. He looked like he was in pain every time he moved. He mentioned that he thought having something to eat might help. Though it sounds strange, usually this does the trick. So eat we did.

I enjoyed my veggie burrito from the carry-out joint across the street, but Senator's quesadillas were the catalyst for a miserable evening. By the second set, he was forced to quickly sneak out to the car to find a nearby drugstore. I manned the recording equipment, in between 1.)noticing that he had not taken the phone, 2.)worrying about his less-than-flawless sense of direction, 3.)pacing in front of the window over the street, 4.)diagnosing his issue as food poisoning, and 5.)wondering how in the world I could go rescue him if he was violently ill somewhere within the surrounding blocks.

My eyes darted down to the street, looking for any sign of our little black car. I glared every time someone claimed one of the few close parking spots that remained. I was tense and beginning to sweat. Just as I was mentally rehearsing how I would demand to drive on the way home, I turned around and he was there. He looked like heck, but he was back, chalky pink bottle of Pepto-Bismol in hand, poor guy.

The set ended and we tore down quickly. There were no arguments about me driving, and amid several emergency stops, we made our way home. Slumped sideways in the passenger seat, looking weak and thin, Senator mumbled, "We'll... laugh about this... in the morning..." I wasn't laughing. I was busy doing the math of how many hours it had been since the accursed jicama had been consumed, and thus, how many more hours of sickness could be expected. Half an hour after getting home, his good-humored prediction came true, though. His entire countenance had changed. He was no longer sick, and we were joking about our adventure while unwinding on the couch. "Apparently the music was so good that I channeled a 1960s jazz junkie," he concluded.

Such was the christening of my summer vacation. The next two weeks contained many more hours of studio time, fixing a leak in our main water pipe, the intermittent construction of our second bathroom by our neighbor, the installation of a ceiling fan to assist the air conditioner in its valiant battle against the relentless summer, physical therapy for injuries not related to any of this, and an outdoor concert where the temperature finally dropped to a tolerable 89°F by midnight. Somehow, through all of this, Senator finished his project, meeting his deadline. He coolly refuted my doubts that we would actually be able to get away. Twenty-four hours before we left for Door County, Wisconsin, I was finally convinced that we would not have to cancel. Sunscreen- check.

The forecast was perfect. We were on the road early, escaping to daytime temperatures in the 70s, with chilly nights in the 50s. Pretty scenery, good conversation, and a few old Jack Benny radio shows helped the drive go by quickly. When I caught my first glimpse of Lake Michigan, I knew it was going to be the refreshing four days I had hoped for.

Upon arriving and greeting our friends, we wasted no time jumping right into recording a podcast. Four years prior, as we sat around a fire at that very same farmhouse in Door County, our friend Bill described his vision for a regular podcast called *On the Lam*. It would be hosted by Bill and Daver (Senator), using a thirty minute format, recorded at various "undisclosed locations". Topics would range from personal stories to commentaries to travelogues to, well, whatever. Occasionally, guests would be invited to sit in.

Two years later, also at the same vacation farmhouse, Bill and Daver recorded their first *On the Lam* session. Throughout the next year, a few more recordings were made as time and compatible schedules allowed, (which was not often). Then Bill got serious. By summer of 2012, he was posting episodes on the internet every Tuesday. This required the recording of many more in order to keep up. Therefore, among visiting, biking, sightseeing, and other activities, they planned to knock out a few more episodes to build up the reserves. On most of these, Bill's wife Marge and I sat in.

During one of the recordings, where just the boys were involved, I was able to duck out for a short bike ride. Despite the open and safe location, Senator was not thrilled about me going out on my own. I understood his concern, because I am never completely at ease while he is riding alone. I told him my route, and that I would only be gone twenty minutes or so. Beyond that, he could send in the Marines if necessary.

Of course I always have more fun when he is with me, but riding alone allowed me to fully drink in and appreciate the fact that we were surrounded by tranquil meadows, a refreshing lake, and, thank God, some cool relief. Though it was early afternoon, a dry breeze kept me comfortable for the entire ride. Short blasts of cool air hit me as I passed through shadows. It probably sounds flaky, but I missed my bike. I had only been on it once all season, and only for about two miles, due to an injury that twisted up some muscles and nerves.* I felt more like myself

---

* I suppose I cannot mention an injury without telling the story behind it, which, incidentally, made it onto one of the *On the Lam* episodes as well. In May, as Senator and I were leaving a record show, walking across the parking lot with stacks of carboard boxes, the strong wind took the lid off of my lightweight box. Instinctively, I ran to retrieve it. Probably due to a premonition, Senator yelled to let it go, but I hated the thought of littering. Not unlike a cartoon, just as I was about to grab it, the wind took it several yards further. I ran again to get it, not realizing that it had moved just beyond the property to a different parking lot. The second lot, unfortunately, was at a very slightly lower elevation, with the added disadvantage

again.

I returned after a short while. Stepping into the kitchen, I waved my presence to Senator, who was still recording with Bill, and nibbled some cheese and crackers. Senator instantly looked more relaxed. Maybe if a couple does not have children, they expend what would be their parental concern toward each other. If so, I can live with that.

After some more time visiting and relaxing, we made a joint motion to go out for pizza. Since everyone was hungry, and no one was worrying about cholesterol on this trip, we ordered the Door County pub requisite, The Munchie Basket. All manner of vegetables that once contained powerful enzymes and nutrients were demoted into wonderfully crispy junk food through the magic of deep frying. *I wonder what this one is. Maybe a mushroom? Or cauliflower? Who knows? Who cares? It's fried!*

When just two morsels o' breaded wonder were left, our server showed up with the pizza. No one wanted to take the last appetizers, but we needed to get the plate out of the way. As a former server, I could tell that our polite deferences were cutting into her time. Literally every second counts when waiting tables. Just as I moved to grab the plate, she jokingly said, "I don't give a damn who eats it. I just need to set down the pizzas!" I love real

---

of a layer of loose gravel. Down I went, hitting the ground hard with my right elbow. Absolutely nothing hurt, but as Senator came running over to help me up, I noticed that my elbow was covered in blood. Sensing that it looked worse than it actually was, I did my best to cover it up with my other hand. My attempt at incognito hemorrhaging failed, but I was able to clean and dress the wound sufficiently. Senator waited outside the ladies' room, worrying and probably requesting a few more guardian angels to offset my tendency toward clumsiness. Eventually all was fine, but the stupid cardboard lid that I so valiantly saved now bears a burgundy/blackish streak that was once part of my blood supply. Henceforth, I rescue no escaping litter.

people.

After dinner we walked the block or so down to the harbor, passing through several 'world shops'. To be clear, world shops are not emporiums of globes or factories staffed with atlas creators. Rather, they are pachouli-scented junk stores, filled with overpriced retro clothing, a bevy of wind chimes of various tone and quality, and scores of other odd trinkets that no one who wasn't in the dizzying throes of a tourist trap would ever consider purchasing.

Still, they are darn fun to browse. In one shop, as I squeezed my way toward the unaffordable skirts, I noticed a display of toy action figures. Where in the world, precisely, did the natives produce plastic replicas of Beethoven (with piano stool), Mozart (serious expression and crazy hair), and Jesus (cross not included)? All I could picture was a bored nine-year old, dragged to the Cape Cod of the Midwest when he really just wanted to go to the waterpark, suddenly perking up with inspiration while passing through the shop. He could now create epic wrestling matches between composers and the Son of God. (Jesus wins, always.)

At another shop the owner was really working his pitch. "Ever been here before?" he greeted each customer individually. "You know, I import from over *twenty* countries," he tempted. "*I sell to other stores...*" Senator explained that the man's comments were code for the fact that he was willing to haggle, but there was nothing that grabbed our attention. Twenty different countries' worth of treasures, and nothing caught my eye. I must be a snob.

When we had exhausted the world, we continued down to the marina, finding a picnic table that overlooked the water. Boats with names suggesting escape and relaxation were idly docked, along with the spice-influenced *Paprika* and *Salt Shaker*. All were missing out on the calm, smooth waters of Green Bay. Naturally, out came the recording device again. In this particular episode, we even captured the cry of a nearby sea gull as it glided across the stereo spectrum.

Another short walk through the woods took us to the aptly named Sunset Beach. The four of us perched on some boulders and gazed west. Other families were there to watch as well. Light blue gave way to darker blue and pink as the sun slipped away quicker than one would have thought it (or rather, Earth) could move. Finally, less than a minute after the last of the orb sank beneath the horizon, the sky lit up in purple, rose, and gold. Everyone applauded.

The only thing left to accomplish on this most non-Monday of Mondays was to enjoy some blueberry cheesecake back at the farmhouse. We were also treated to a rare and special viewing of a home movie featuring Bill and his friends in a crazy Joliet escapade circa 1970. Traveling further back in time, we also delved into another of the 1940s serials that have captivated both Bill and Senator. This time it was *King of the Rocket Men*. And just in case you are completely enthralled with Chapter 1 of this serial, take comfort in knowing that there are eleven more action-packed episodes, plus two more sequels. That's a lot of rockets, my friend.

*   *   *

Tuesday morning we all woke up early to coordinate with the ferry schedules for a trip to somewhat remote Rock Island. The state park island, which sits just northeast of Washington Island, which sits just north of Door County, was once owned by wealthy inventor Chester H. Thordarson. He kept its 900 acres rustic and beautiful, with a few additions of Icelandic-inspired stone buildings. To this day, no motor vehicles or bikes are allowed on the island, so don't go if you don't want to walk.

We drove to the first ferry point and parked the cars. Bill and Senator unhooked the bikes from their car racks, and Marge and I went to the booth to buy tickets. It was early, and we were the only ones in line. Marge was casually talking with the ticket attendant, who mentioned that we had plenty of time to catch the next ferry. I, standing behind Marge, jokingly butted in. "Hurry it up, wouldya? I'm in line hee-yah!" The poor man looked stunned, not realizing that we were together. He seemed relieved when Marge and I started chatting. For a moment, he must have thought I was a real jerk.

Our bikes were loaded onto the ferry, and we took our seats on the deck above. 360 degrees of clean, deep blue water was the setting for the next podcast. These shows were getting addicting. As tiny uninhabited islands floated by and Washington Island approached, we covered various random topics over the steady hum of the ferry's engine. Why couldn't someone just pay us to ramble our thoughts into a microphone while being surrounded by such natural beauty? I could give up teaching for that.

The ride took about thirty minutes, so we finished up our episode just as the boat reached the landing. We then shuffled down the narrow staircase and claimed our bikes, amazed at the ideal weather. From the landing, it was an eight-mile bike to the second ferry, which was positioned on the opposite side of the island. Farms, a few small businesses, a couple of churches, and a café came in and out of view. The loudest noise I heard while riding was a rooster's crow.

Just as I was getting tired from the up and down of riding over the hills, we reached the ferry parking lot. A dozen or so cars were parked there, including those of people who had camped on Rock Island. We found a bike rack and locked our bikes to it, although I noticed that no one else bothered to do so. That was reassuring.

We had reached a new depth of casual, even beyond that of mainland Door County. The ferry to Rock Island could only hold about twenty people. As we watched it dock, we saw people unloading all of their necessary camping gear, which had just been sitting on the boat's floor. When everyone was off,

Marge and I asked a worker where we could buy tickets. "I have 'em here," was his simple response. We paid and he told us to sit anywhere.

"Don't we need a return ticket?" I asked, halfway thinking that it wouldn't necessarily be a bad thing to be stranded in such a beautiful place.

"Nope." Again, simplicity. I guess they figured that one must have paid for a round trip ticket in order to get to the island, so they were okay with bringing you back.* We found our seats and watched two or three other parties climb aboard, including a small black lab, who must have thought he died and went to doggy heaven.

When everyone was aboard, the ferry slowly pulled out. The man who had taken our tickets stood at the rear of the boat, in the aisle between the two rows of seats. He looked disapprovingly at the situation, and then asked for volunteers to move from the starboard to the port side. Enough people did and he smiled in thanks, grateful that we would not capsize.

The ride was only about fifteen minutes long, but it felt like we had traveled to a much more remote region. A large stone boathouse with arched inlets came into view. Except for restrooms, it was the only building we could see. The beach led to a meadow covered with wildflowers. Beyond the meadow was a steep, wooded hill.

Before a hike to the lighthouse, we took a break at a picnic table under a tree. We unpacked some snacks, and, of course, the recorder. With the sapphire blue lake in the background, we passed another half hour storytelling and laughing in front of the microphone. Then we got up to fill our water bottles, and we were off again.

The retired man who volunteered at the island told us that it was about 1.25 miles to the lighthouse. We figured it

---

* (provided you were at the landing by the 4:15pm curfew)

would be a relatively easy walk along the beach since lighthouses were, after all, along shores. Instead, we found ourselves sweating our way up a very steep grade, over a rocky path through the woods. The water seemed to move farther and farther away as we ascended. The hike was strenuous, making the mile-and-a-quarter feel like three miles.

When we finally reached the lighthouse, we took a quick break under another tree. It was an average-sized lighthouse, in good condition. Senator and I stepped inside to take a short tour. The current lighthouse keeper's daughter instructed us to take off our shoes and wait for her father, who would be down in a moment. I did not realize that there were still light tenders in this day and age. I suppose the light is automated, but given the remote location and the logistics involved in reaching the lighthouse, keepers stay for week-long shifts to give tours, and then they return to the mainland.

We toured the six rooms of living quarters, learning about the families who had lived there, and about the seven anonymous bodies that were buried in the nearby cemetery after being washed ashore through the years. Then we climbed a very narrow staircase, (which was really more like a ladder,) to the actual light room. The tiny platform was only three or four stories above the ground, but it was enough of a difference to open up the view of Lake Michigan and Michigan's Upper Peninsula to three times as wide as what we had seen below. We stared for a moment or two, and then I turned to go back downstairs. Looking downward, it seemed even steeper. I paused for a moment to determine my strategy. Remembering how I had wiped out six weeks earlier, I was taking no chances. Like a little old lady, I shimmied my way backward down each step, clutching the previous step in my hands.

Rejoining Bill and Marge, we practically ran back down the trail. It wasn't that we were late; it was just that gravity was now on our side. The path that had seemed suspiciously like three miles now seemed like a mere block. It's funny how the body and mind fool each other.

Because the walk back had been so easy, we just made it onto the earlier of two ferries. Not surprisingly, our bikes were right where we had left them on Washington Island... and so were all of the unlocked bikes. We pedaled hard, pushing it for a partly uphill 6½ miles, and then stopped for ice cream. The sugar high carried us the final two miles to the ferry landing.

There was no podcasting on the ferry ride back. We had biked and hiked a combined total of about twenty miles, and everyone was enjoying the quiet break. I closed my eyes to rest, but popped them open to the sounds of obnoxious children running around the deck. A family of at least six kids and two immature adults for some reason deemed it a good idea to play hide-and-seek on the boat. They squeezed their way past annoyed passengers, running around and almost falling down the stairs a few times. *I know a great hiding place*, I thought, looking over the side of the boat.

When we had all had enough of the vermin, I did the only thing I could think of to repel rowdy young boys. Turning to face Senator, I grabbed his head and pressed my lips hard to his, going for an all-out sloppy kiss that threatened to use tongue if one more kid came running past us. It worked perfectly. We were not disturbed for the remainder of the crossing. It's true-- love *can* overcome anything.

Once we got off the ferry, hunger set in. Though we were somewhat disheveled and far from dressed up, Door County is easygoing enough that we decided to stop for a bite to eat. We got a table at a comfortable Mexican-American place, and I excused myself to the restroom to conduct necessities and put myself together a bit. As I stepped inside the bathroom, I laughed at the comical site. Across from the toilet sat three extra dining room chairs, all facing the throne. I assumed that someone had decided to ditch them in the bathroom to get them out of the way until needed. As one took care of business however, it looked like an audience could file in at any moment. I could picture a family cramming into the room. "Mind if we wait here for our table?..."

Dinner was tasty, but I was really anticipating a shower and a nap. Senator and I had been tired from the moment we woke up, and exercise in the fresh air had only added to the lethargic feeling. He showered first and got dressed. As I was finishing my shower, I heard him announce that we had a problem. "There's a wasp in our room."

Shoot! All I wanted to do was sleep, but now I was on high alert. We had to kill the thing, or at least let it out before bedtime that night. Of course it kept wiggling around on the light's hardware, staying just out of reach of any flat surface that would render its disposal easy.

We debated how to go about the attack without having it backfire on us. I volunteered to be the swatter, but Senator said I was too slow, so I just stood there dripping in a towel, narrating my gut feelings, as Senator acquired a broom, a dustpan, and a shoe. "No, I don't think you should strike there. It's too risky. Wait. Okay, he's between the door and the frame now."

That sucker stayed just where we couldn't see him. We each watched from opposite sides of the open door, convinced that he had to come out sooner or later. "Not yet..." Finally the winged menace was lured into a false sense of security. He crept onto a flat surface to his doom. "Now! And hit hard!" SMACK! He fell from the wall, but Senator hit him another three or four times just to be safe. After working hard to outsmart a bug, we both fell asleep.

Waking up from a nap at twilight is a little surreal, but eventually we emerged from our fog long enough to contribute to another podcast. With the help of more blueberry cheesecake, we saw our way through two more episodes of *King of the Rocket Men*. By the time we fell asleep again, our flying hero had punched out a dozen more bad guys, used his ray gun rather effectively, and postponed any threat to Earth yet again.

*   *   *

Wednesday began with sleeping in a bit later, but the smell of fresh coffee drifting up the stairs, and the chance to spend another day by clear water were motivation not to doze for too long. Despite a mildly disapproving look from my boyfriend, I bargained for another short solitary bike ride while the others ate breakfast. Again the air was so clean, and I saw several other bikers taking advantage of the beautiful morning, too. The faster I rode, the better I felt. Before long I was pulling back into the driveway, my wild freedom run successfully concluded.

As I sipped a cup of coffee, Marge asked what we wanted to do that day. "Well, anything is fine," I began, "but if no one has any other plans, I'd love to get back to Cave Point." Bill and Marge jumped on the idea. Senator had no memory of the gorgeous park with the rocky bluffs and long, uncrowded beach, but I remembered how much we had both enjoyed it. We decided to make the most of our time there by first stopping for some picnic supplies.

On the way to Cave Point, we also stopped at a library to check email. Senator was pleased to discover that the recorded material he had been working on for the past month had safely arrived in Poland, despite warnings that customs officials there often rejected such packages. That was a great relief. Now on to the picnic.

The Door County Bakery is home to the famous Corsica Loaf, a large homemade bread that is freshly baked each day on a bed of olive oil, inside a European stone oven. Sound tempting? Into the picnic bag it went. The bakery also sells other artisan products, but they were not currently stocking the highlight of any picnic involving Marge and Senator-- their beloved pickled garlic. Clearly, no feast could be had without the delicious, smelly little cloves, so we decided to try another market down the road.

Hence, Koepsel's. Inside this farm market*, we were greeted by endless rows of jams, cherries, home-baked treats, cheeses, all things pickled, and more. I believe we actually all stared in awe before grabbing hand baskets to shop. Even more impressive than the selection was the quality of ingredients and the reasonable prices. We had stumbled onto a gem.

As I perused apple and pumpkin butters, I overhead a serious discussion between Marge and Senator. They had to choose between two different types of pickled garlic. After much deliberation regarding color, texture, and other aspects of garlic that normal people do not notice, they selected their beloved jar. Needless to say, none of us were getting bit by vampires that night.

With all of the necessary components of a grand Door County picnic, we drove to Cave Point. Several families were there enjoying the day, but we still managed to stake out the best picnic table. Shaded by a large tree, our spot overlooked Lake Michigan as it crashed into the cove. We carefully laid out the buffet, balancing items on one side so we could all sit on the opposite bench to take in the view. It was (garlic) breathtaking. I have decided that it is one of my favorite places in the Midwest. If you get the chance, Reader, hop up the west coast of Lake Michigan and pay this county park a visit. Just don't tell too many people about it...

After another podcast, (peppered with Koepsel's endorsements), we took the path down to the shore. Cave Point boasts a wide rocky beach, without any of that pesky sand. Oh yes, I realize that I've just offended the coastal constituents, but I have no use for the hot, clingy grit. Rocks are endlessly

---

*   in business since 1958

superior.*

Because of varying wave patterns, some lower spots in the rocks held pools of trapped water. Wading in these felt like stepping into bath water. Further out in the open water, it gradually got cooler. It was like a natural thermostat, allowing you to choose your own temperature. We all took our time, sometimes walking together and chatting, and sometimes separating into private investigations of local plant and animal life.

When we stumbled upon an inviting carved out nook behind some sea grass, we agreed it was time to record another podcast. We sat within view of the lake, but we were unnoticed by other beach walkers. Soon another chatty half hour had passed. Taking our time and dawdling whenever possible, we walked toward the parking lot to leave.

At the house, we dozed off one by one. How low-key walking and talking can wear a person out I will never know. If we were this lazy in our daily lives, we would never accomplish anything. We must have silently given our bodies permission to regenerate and recharge.

*   *   *

The final planned event for the Door County trip was the long awaited Spooky Podcast. The last time we were at the farmhouse, Bill had shown us the old, windowless basement. While useful under threat of tornado, it admittedly had a creepy vibe to it, especially at night. With this in mind, at some point Senator had the idea to record a podcast down there late at night.

As a precursor to spooky podcasting, we sat outside around a crackling fire, recording yet another episode. The sky was black, but it seemed like there were more stars than background. This session was not scary, but it did involve a

---

*As my grandma points out, "They [rocks] must be important. After all, when we went to the moon, that's what we brought back!"

rousing campfire song solo by Bill. The tune had something to do with a fox hunting a goose, so I suppose if you had deep sympathies with fowl, it could have been spine-tingling.

When the last log had died out, we moved the party indoors. Apparently there was an unspoken rule that Spooky Podcast could not begin before midnight, so Bill fired up a few more chapters of *King of the Rocket Men*. Unlike the Ramones, I did want to go down to the basement, but there would be plenty of time for that later. For the moment, I was absorbing a useful education on the fundamentals of flying in a rocket suit, thanks to Commando Cody:

> #1 To prepare to save innocent people or defeat bad guys, turn the on/off button on the chest panel to the "ON" position.
> #2 To take off, use a running start and then jump, preferably from an off-screen trampoline.
> #3 To increase altitude, select "UP" from the up/down button on the chest panel.
> #4 To decrease altitude, select "DOWN" from the up/down button on the chest panel.
> #5 To land, move into a vertical position, so the feet can drop down to the ground at will. (Can be tricky.)
> #6 To save power for the next necessary flight to save innocent people or defeat bad guys, turn the on/off button on the chest panel to the "OFF" position.

There was no ominous bell to toll the dark hour, but the microwave clock said 12:20, so I guess that was just as good. Marge lit a candle, and Bill grabbed a flashlight that could double as a weapon. The four of us filed down the stairs and found our previously arranged seats. The recorder was set on a stool in the middle of our circle. Senator switched on the device, and Bill switched off the flashlight.

We wailed an impromptu, "Wooo-oooh" in unison. As

our eyes adjusted to the darkness, I wondered how we would explain this scene if, by chance, the owner of the farmhouse happened to stop by. Perhaps we could turn it back on him and ask what he was doing creeping around in the middle of the night. Honestly, we were all old enough to have kids going to slumber parties doing something like this, yet here we were, four grown adults, sitting in a basement sharing tales of strange and mysterious encounters.

Because Spooky Podcasts have no time limit, I believe we went well over our half hour allotment. No apparitions were seen in the basement, but I was intrigued by an antique table the lurked in the shadows. And exactly what occurred in those odd little tales? You will just have to listen to *On the Lam*[*] to find out.

*   *   *

The sun peeked through the outdated shade in the bedroom window. It was time to get ready to go home. Our getaway had gotten away too fast. I rolled out of bed and mentally planned everything that had to be done in the next hour or so. Senator squinted his eyes open, trying to focus before sitting up.

When everything was loaded into the car, we sat for a few moments with our friends. Outside the picture window, two blue jays pecked their breakfast from the feeder. The previous year we had had to cancel our trip to Door County, but this year made up for it. We said our good-byes, interrupted by brainstorms of where we could bike or hike next year if we returned. Under another bright blue sky, we left Fish Creek.

As is my habit, I spent a portion of the ride home planning the next trip. This was not so much due to my obsession as the fact that we would be leaving again in just one

---

[*] Look for it on Facebook. Or just Google it if Facebook is obsolete by the time you read this. Or just envision it if the internet is obsolete by the time you read this.

week. I think it was the closest we had ever scheduled two vacations. To my notes I added the word "sunglasses" to remind me to replace the broken pair that was now dangling from my right ear. In order to fit another trip in, Senator would have to work the next seven days straight, while I prepared and packed.

"What did you say?" I realized Senator had spoken to me, jarring me from my thoughts. "You want to squeeze in another recording session the night before we leave?..." Sure. Why not? And then I dozed off.

Chapter 3
Taken for Granite: Late July 2012

Five books into this shindig, I suppose I should give you an appropriate piece of background information about myself. I am a native New Hampshirite who had the strange fortune to be born in Illinois. Somewhere back in the year I'm-not-telling-you-when, a stork (or *stahk*) got his signals crossed. Whereas he should have begun his descent just north of Concord (or *Concud*), landing gently over the White Mountains, at just that moment, a record-breaking wind gust rushed forth from Mount Washington, sweeping the poor beladen bird far to the west. Eventually I was dropped in Joliet, or as we call it, Prison City.[*]

This turned out to be a fortuitous turn of events, as I was born to the two greatest parents I can imagine. Later, in the same geographic area (or *airier*), I met my perfect partner and foil, Senator. At that point, I had obtained everything worth obtaining from Illinois. While jobs, a home, and recording jazz[†] have kept us here and continue to keep us here for the immediate future, we continue to dream about someday

---

[*] Yes, there is an internationally famous prison there, but that's not why we call it that.
[†] The order of priority of these factors changes on a regular basis...

relocating. My dream is to Live Free or Die, which is why in July 2011, I began a twelve month countdown until we could visit New Hampshire again.

If you have read my first book, you may remember that Senator and I traveled through New Hampshire on our first trip together. A planned urban weekend in New York City resulted in an unplanned rural road trip through the New England countryside. What I remember about New Hampshire is seeing rolling hills dotted with farms, small but steady white churches with steeples piercing a blue sky, and crumbling but still respected graveyards. And I think we drank some coffee, too.

Since then, I have continued to fan my romanticization of New Hampshire, occasionally adding solid facts and data to the picture. Apart from the obvious beautiful scenery and far more comfortable summers, my research has taught me a few tidbits of information that continue to attract me to The Granite State:

> 1. New Hampshire state legislators only represent about 3,250 constituents each. That means there are a lot of them. At an *annual* salary of $100 per pop though, they come cheap.
> 2. Natives place a high value on privacy. Friendly, yes. Helpful, yes. Nosy, no. Leave them alone and they'll leave you alone. Not unlike moose.
> 3. They love books. Real ones-- the kind that don't take batteries.
> 4. New Hampshire has no state income tax or state sales tax. By comparison, I come from a state where the last two governors are in jail for big-deal/dirty- money corruption, and the current governor ran on a platform to raise taxes... and won!

So you begin to see my devotion. More importantly, Senator began to see my devotion. That is why, after working Thursday morning, (which followed three hours of sleep, which followed a long night of recording, which followed a long day of managing retail,) he joined me in a venture east. I volunteered to drive first.

Sometime around 11:30pm, we agreed that we should look for a hotel. We took some pride in the fact that we had made it all the way past Cleveland, but we did not realize that doing so put us in an odd gap between decent accommodations. Not having had occasion to study the far northeastern reaches of Ohio, I did not understand that there are not many hotels from which to choose. Those that exist are either fully booked or less than desirable. In both cases, they are overpriced.

We eventually settled for a Ramada and went inside together. The lobby seemed clean, and the woman behind the desk was friendly, if a bit unprofessional. *Hey, they all can't act like office execs. And who really needs all of their teeth, anyway?*

She proceeded to check us in, and then paused as I signed the receipt. "Man, my dad's gonna' kill me when he sees what I did to my hair!" She couldn't pass for a day under forty. I instinctively glanced up at her chaotic dye job. Dark streaks settled on a rusty orange compromise with fried blondish locks underneath. "I mean, I just wanted to do it, but it turned out different. But I think it's okay?..."

I wasn't sure if we were supposed to nod in solidarity, look away, or help her thumb the yellow pages for an emergency stylist. So we smiled stupidly. Her hair speech segued randomly into a recitation of the necessary hotel information. Continental breakfast was available from 6:00-10:00am. Our room was around the right corner, on the second floor. "And, you know, there's a pool..." she added doubtfully with a half-grin, as if we all knew that no one ever bothered to swim in it, for various reasons.

We thanked her and went around the outside of the building to the wing which contained our room. Though it was a nonsmoking section, the entryway before the hall smelled like its previous occupants had been terrified that they might not get a chance to smoke again before checkout. They must have smoked their entire pack in preparation. If our room smelled anything like that, we would turn around and leave.

As it turned out, our room did not smell like cigarettes. The dingy early-80s pastel walls weren't exactly dirty, but the entire room was as damp as a cave.[*] Apparently exhaustion had set in enough for us to agree that the room was just this side of acceptable. After all, there were no bugs, and we would be on the road again in nine hours anyway. Just to be safe, I zipped up our suitcase to keep the moisture off of our clothes.

The next morning the air hung heavy in the room. It seemed even damper, if that is possible. We both ached from a mostly sleepless night, and perhaps from the temporary onset of rheumatic fever. Then and there a new family rule was established. We would no longer drive so far that our judgment was impaired when deeming what was acceptable in a room. Motion carried. Adding insult to injury, it ended up being more expensive than several other wonderful inns at which we had stayed in the past. Supply and demand wins again.

*   *   *

We kicked off the drive around the southern portion of Lake Erie with some good old fashioned long distance AM radio. According to a weather report from two hundred miles away in Ontario, it would be a lovely summer day. Or, if we cared to drive an extra five hours out of our way, another station cordially invited us to attend their community picnic. At least, that's what I think the man said. Every time he started to speak in English, he would get excited and slip back into Italian. Somewhere in Ohio or Pennsylvania or New York or Ontario or Quebec, a wonderful time of pasta and merriment was ensuing. Random

---

[*] Yes it is a cliché, thank you very much. Sometimes nothing else will do. You see, that's why they are clichés.

French and Polish programs killed another hour or so as we drove into New York.

Hours of driving went smoothly until we got off the interstate in eastern New York. We made the mistake of cutting through Saratoga Springs before making our way into Vermont. Block after block of a downtown historic district that any glossy brochure would describe as "quaint" sucked in tourists by the hundreds. Aahhh! We had been spoiled by clipping along uninterrupted, but we suddenly found ourselves at a standstill.

Mobs of middle-aged city denizens 'got away from it all' by shopping exclusive boutiques and sipping on unheard of wines from exotic places like Erie, Pennsylvania. Outdoor cafés allowed the tourists to enjoy the local scenery, namely the rest of us poor saps stuck in cars that crawled their main street. As we nibbled our homemade apple crisp that I had brought along, I wondered how much I could sell my desserts for if I declared them 'artisan sweetbreads'.

Eventually Saratoga Springs released us and we crossed into Vermont. Immediately the Green Mountains were in view and everything felt more relaxed. I invite debate on this point, but in my humble opinion, there is a subtle but marked difference the moment one crosses into New England. Suddenly trees are a priority, and the first covered bridge you pass says, "It'll get done later. Come enjoy the stream for a while. It's running fast this year."

We exited Route 4 toward the small town of Castleton. In the late afternoon, we checked into our reserved bed and breakfast. It was so quiet on the home's property that you could almost hear the butterflies. I couldn't help but be a little jealous of the bountiful gardens of blooming perennials. Back home new sections of my gardens were dying weekly due to drought, despite my attempts to save them.

We stepped into our room tentatively, in light of the previous night's humid repose. We were relieved to find it clean, comfortable, cozy, and DRY. Senator sat down and rested his eyes while I arranged a few items on the vanity. I was lost in the contentment of actually being in my beloved New England.

Then he popped up and went to the window. "Hey V, check this out..." He opened the window and a light, clear, DRY breeze came in. "I think we can actually sleep with the window open!" he announced excitedly. Yes, I vaguely remembered doing such a thing. Recently at home though, the mere thought of leaving a window open could send a body into a considerable sweat. We had lost count of how many 100+° days we had hibernated through. Fresh air had become a special treat. In fact, we took an airy nap to test it out.

After a long doze we were both hungry. I told Senator I would be happy with a sandwich or something simple. Heck, a slice of toast would have felt perfect at that moment. Nope. He informed me that we were going to go out to dinner and splurge and relax. (So far, Vermont was as great as I had remembered.) He leafed through a few of the menus of local restaurants. The Blue Cat's mushroom-garlic ravioli in white wine cream sauce convinced me that he was right.

* * *

The next morning at breakfast we chatted with a few of the other guests and our host. Through the brief conversation, we learned two pieces of potentially useful information.[*] First of all, New England adults like to play outside. Almost everyone in the room had hiked Mount Washington-- not an easy trek-- at least once. Some had hiked it several times. Everyone raved about the views and scenery, and no one complained about the exertion. This is encouraging if we ever choose to move to the

---

[*] These were in addition to another vital fact we had verified while walking around the property the previous evening. Gardens, and specifically tomatoes like we love to grow in the Midwest, do thrive in New England as well. Good to know!

region. We have grand plans to stay physically active well into our 80s, at least.

The second thing we learned is that New Englanders don't get out much. Out of their corner of the United States, that is. To our amusement, everyone seemed impressed by the fact that we had driven there from Illinois. This turned out to be the normal reaction wherever we went that week, and it was backed up by our observations. If we saw out-of-state license plates, they were never from more than a state or two away. We were reverse pioneers, foreigners who had come east from a far away land... even farther than Pittsburgh!

Although, few pioneers visit castles. After leaving the other guests in awe of our vast motoring capabilities, we traveled to the nearby town (debatable) of Proctor. During the latter half of the 1800s, a Vermont doctor went to England to study. In addition to medicine, he mastered the study of an older and much wealthier aristocrat, eventually bringing her back to Vermont as his bride. Naturally, she insisted on the construction of a mansion unrivaled by anything the local cows had seen. At a cost of $1,300,000[*], the self-proclaimed castle was complete. They could have easily shaved a few bucks off the immense total if the couple had not insisted that everything (building materials, furniture, livestock, etc.) be imported from Europe. This included the English brick, which was the exact wrong choice in exteriors when it came to the four distinct New England seasons. Oh, and then they got divorced.

Our very animated tour guide took us through the rooms of the first and second floor, pointing out elaborate woodwork and extravagance at every turn. For example, have you ever seen a window over a fireplace? Probably not, as the chimney tends to be a necessity. At Wilson Castle, however, you can see just that, as the owners had a split chimney designed to go around a

---

[*] in 1870s cdollars!

very intricate hand-painted glass. When the morning sun backlights it, the scene is brilliant. As are the many stained glass windows throughout the home, including the acid-etched portrait of a knight.

Outside the castle, you can walk the grounds. Three sides of the acreage are wooded, and the fourth side offers an expansive view of a meadow at the foot of the Green Mountains. You can also take a very short jog over to the cage, which once housed domestically useless creatures like peacocks. Apparently, everything in this place had to be gorgeous.

We wrapped up our visit to Wilson Castle, taking advantage of their rare photography-permitted-and-even-encouraged policy. Heading east again, we crossed the river into New Hampshire. The heavens opened up, and there were rainbows! No there weren't, but it was just as beautiful as I had remembered as we climbed to the higher elevation of the White Mountains.

Our first stop, in order to do this thing right, was a cheese shop. Harman's Cheese & Country Store[*] has been dealing in regional homemade and all-natural goodies since 1955. We stocked up on cheese, crackers, salad dressing, and yes, pickled garlic. *This stuff must have a cult following.* This little red shop with the old wooden floors is also home to just about any product you can make using maple syrup. Maple candies or cookies you could get anywhere. We opted for a spicy maple mustard instead, and it did not disappoint. Slightly confuse, yes, but disappoint, no.

With our picnic sack significantly packed, we drove down to Franconia Notch State Park. It was too late in the day to start hiking, but there was plenty of time to devour a picnic dinner. We found a table and spread out our odd assortment of Vermont and New Hampshire comestibles. As we nibbled and planned

---

[*] The name says it all.

the next few days, a chipmunk and a few large black birds patrolled the area. We never did figure out if they were ravens or just very well fed crows.

Then a mosquito buzzed by. Hhmmm. I had planned the entire trip based on a leap of faith that we could explore the woods and water without being attacked by the little vampires. Knowing Senator's inexplicable appeal to mosquitoes, it was quite a leap of faith indeed. A battalion of bloodsuckers could also be a deal breaker in any future plans to make our homestead in New Hampshire. I glared at the demon as Senator shooed it away.

We finished our garlic-cheddar-rosemary-maple-mustard feast and drove to the inn where we would spend the next four nights. The Arts & Crafts style two-story sat back from the road, and just far enough away from the small downtown to be peaceful. We stepped into the long enclosed porch, already feeling comfortable. Inside the front door, no one seemed to be around. We glanced around, and then noticed a note on the desk.

Next to an old desk phone* was a note instructing us to call the indicated phone number if no one was there. So I did. "Hi," I began, trying to invent an appropriate introduction. "Uh, we have a reservation at the Wilderness Inn, and a note said to call this number(?)"

At the other end of the line was our host, sounding busy, but genuinely glad to hear from us. "Oh, great! Well, we're out swimming at Mirror Lake. So, would you mind letting yourselves in?" This was a different sort of check-in process from what we were used to, but at least it did not involve an analysis of a hair dye job gone bad.

"Sure, we can do that," I shrugged, invisibly to her. She then directed me to the desk drawer. Inside was a key with our

---

* Remember squiggly cords?

room number on it. I looked across the room to see the filled coffee pot and mini-fridge where she said it would be. We concluded our conversation and settled into our room, making a mental note that the crime rate must be low enough for people to leave home and belongings exposed while they took the afternoon off for a casual swim.

All that remained on the agenda was killing some time before viewing fireworks later that night. Among our wanderings we stumbled onto a local park, which happened to be hosting a senior citizen jazz band in its gazebo. We listened for a while, smiling as the drummer, who was surely somebody's grandma, tapped out her signature solo. Recording international jazz innovators is one thing, but sitting with a crowd of smiling and truly content small town locals is another kind of blessing.

Still full from our late picnic, we skipped dinner in lieu of some homemade ice cream. A few birds looked at us jealously. Thankfully, none attacked my cone. I even finished the whole scoop before it melted. At home that would have meant in less than two minutes, given the extreme heat. Here, in the cool of the evening, we took our time.

Enjoying the casual pace, we drove to a resort that hosted fireworks twice each week at 9:00pm during the summer. Making our best guess as to where the show would occur, we parked the car in a neighboring lot. With the windows down we waited, discussing the trails we would hike the next day. As the last of the daylight slipped behind the mountains, I eagerly anticipated the show. It had been several years since we had seen fireworks together.

At 8:55pm, the night was still quiet. "Well, they should get going any minute," I commented, "unless I have the wrong night." I was joking, but as soon as I said it, I began to second-guess myself. *Could I really have done something that dumb?* I wondered. *Wouldn't be the first time,* I answered myself.

I grabbed my travel papers and read my notes.

"Fireworks Sunday- 9pm". I ticked off the days we had been gone in my head. *Friday, Saturday, Sunday...* Then it hit me. Though this was the third day on the road, we had left on Thursday, a day earlier than our usual vacation departures. Ergo, it was Saturday. Ergo, fireworks would begin promptly in twenty-four hours and three minutes. "Oh, geez! I really did get the wrong night!" I blurted out. We both had a good laugh about it, but I still feel pretty dumb about that one. At least our dress rehearsal was successful.

*   *   *

The next morning after breakfast, we hopped onto The Kanc[*], local short for the Kancamagus Highway. With miles of scenic views in the midst of the White Mountains, it lived up to its reputation as one of America's most beautiful byways. It is also the access point for numerous trails and campgrounds. A few miles into the route, we chose our first hike.

The Forest Discovery trail parking lot was empty. That was either a really good or really bad sign, but it was only a one mile loop, so we decided to use it as our initiation into this great national forest. I finished lacing up my boots as Senator read me the warning sign at the trailhead. "Warning- High bee/wasp activity." Bees and wasps? I was too busy gauging the mosquito situation. I was very aware of the fact that the next few days could be relegated to indoor Yahtzee games instead of outdoor activities, if the mosquitoes attacked. Now I had to worry about hoards of stingers, too? There was only one way to find out.

Even though we took our time, the mile loop was a quick trail. Most importantly, not one mosquito, bee, wasp, or pest of any sort was anywhere in sight. We had no idea what the sign was referring to. The air was clean, the shade was cool, we were ready to move on, and New Hampshire wasn't out of the running for Possible Places to Move.

---

* also, The Kank

Our next stop, also accessed from The Kanc, was the Greeley Ponds Trail. This parking lot was full, and it was a weekend day, so we thought we might be in for a crowded, touristy walk. Not so. We only encountered a few people as we hiked, mainly uphill, for about a mile and a half, on a rocky and rooty[*] path.

In two places we paused to decide which way to go. The map on the sign did not match the map I was using. Hhmmm. I thought maybe we should go right. Senator had a stronger opinion in favor of left. He was correct. Later, at another fork, our choices were reversed. This time I was correct. So it turned out to be a good thing that we hiked together, and that whichever one of us felt he/she was right spoke up to defend it.

When we reached the pond, we took a short break to look over its calm horizon. In the distance a man was photographing the backdrop, or us. It was hard to tell. Anxious to see more, we started the return trip.

About ten minutes into the walk, we encountered a Japanese family who looked a little lost. They seemed to be debating the same route options that we had. Happy to help fellow hikers, I pointed the appropriate direction and explained, "It's only ten minutes that way to the pond." They smiled and nodded thanks, and I nodded in return, feeling very content with the world, the forest, and myself.

"You know they have no idea what you just said, don't you?" Senator asked.

"Yeah. I know." Down the trail we went.

I will pause here to say that, if you ever plan to hike along any of the trails that cross or begin at the Kancamagus Highway, spend the time to create a good map before you go. Why not just print one out, you may wonder? Because each map contradicts all others. Instead, you must research several of them, and then

---

* (a natural consequence of 800,000 acres of woodlands)

spread your findings out on your living room floor (preferably with a good cup of coffee nearby), carefully and tactfully synthesizing them into One. My theory is that the locals are doing their best to strike a delicate balance between attracting tourism dollars and keeping a few natural secrets to themselves. But I am learning their ways.

Taking a side road off of The Kanc led us to several more trails. By this point, I had given up finding our intended hikes on the map, so we opted to drive until we "saw something that sounded pretty". What that meant exactly, I had no idea. Eventually we saw a sign for Ripley Falls. Falls are good. We parked the car and started another steep walk.

In fact, it was a very steep walk. The only time we were not climbing or descending was the hundred feet or so that followed some train tracks. Though we took our time and moved safely up the sometimes muddy trail, I was a little surprised at the dropoff. At least there were a lot of trees to hang on to if necessary. Live free or die.

When we reached the top, the water pounded down in a long cascade over a glassy rock face. The sun was bright as it bounced off the mirrorlike surface. At the bottom, the water splashed around between some large boulders before dissipating into a babbling brook. Senator tried to pose us for a photo or two, but we could not maneuver into a spot that would work with the sun's position. From previous ventures, we had learned our limits when straddling rocks in streams.

On the drive back to our inn we took a longer detour for another view of the mountains. Yes, you could argue that big hills with trees from one angle look the same as big hills with trees from another angle, and you would be right, to an extent. The object in such trips is not necessarily to see something different; it is to experience the vastness of it. If you have ever driven a large section of desert, you know what I mean. It is invigorating to see how much rugged landscape has managed to hold its own—in part thanks to protective acts of Congress—against human progress. I find it very hopeful and positive.

Nearing the little town where we were staying, Senator spotted a used book store. Actually, it was more of a used book/ yard ornament/ antique/ stuff store. Like all great independent bookshops, there were plenty of books crammed everywhere, vaguely organized into narrow aisles that would soon become death traps in a fire. Of course, we couldn't get out without buying a few books. When, through casual conversation the owner found out that Senator was a YES fan, he gave us a discount. The books had nothing to do with the band, but the man figured he had found a kindred spirit, and that was enough for him.

After a shower, a good solid nap, and some enchiladas outside in view of the mountains, it was time to go hunting. It was our second night in the White Mountains, and despite several warning signs about car-moose collisions, our sum total of moose sightings stood firm at exactly zero. I had read a single line in a guidebook that hinted at a certain known moose hangout, so we thought we would give it a try. Thus, the Great Moose Stakeout had begun.

The plan was to catch a moose or two while they sauntered down to a certain pond in the early evening hours. There was great scientific reason behind our choice of time and place. We chose evening because at home deer were always prancing around in the dusk. Moose, therefore, being large mammals of occasionally similar habits, should be most visible after dinner. As for the locale, we turned onto the now-familiar Kanc, since it had a solid reputation of man-moose disasters. Shortly afterward, we stopped the car at Lily Pond.

From 7:00pm-8:00pm we sat in our vehicle, alternately scanning the horizon for moose who were scanning the horizon for us. Even at this time of day it was comfortably dry, and no mosquitoes troubled us. *Man, I love this place!* We talked about the area and watched the clouds, wondering if it would sprinkle that night. All was peaceful. So peaceful, in fact, that no moose bothered to break the silence. Better luck next time, kids.

There was still one more event to watch for. This time it truly *was* fireworks night. We once again parked the car in a lot near the resort, in déjà vu fashion. A few other cars had the same idea, and we all faced the mountains, ready for a good free show. The lady from the SUV next to us summed it up. "I called an' asked the guy about the fireworks. He said he didn't think they were open to the public. So I says 'What are ya' gonna' do? Make everyone else look down?' " Well stated.

A few minutes after 9:00pm, the first explosion rocked the mountains. At that instant we both realized what a unique experience it was to hear fireworks in a valley. The boom echoed for several seconds afterward, bouncing around each hill. A long pause followed.

Just as we began to wonder if the *fireworks* show was actually a *firework* show, several more screeches sounded, sending up blasts of brilliant color. Then there was another long pause, perhaps for dramatic effect? More likely their timing needed some adjustment. At completely irregular intervals, large pyrotechnic displays wowed guests and public alike, followed by periods of dead silence. "Hhmmm. Unusual, but good. I guess that's it." As we were about to start up the car to leave, the grand finale filled the sky with multi-layered explosions and their residual smoke trails. Rather an impressive show... and much better than the night before.

*　　　*　　　*

It had drizzled during the night, but as we finished our breakfast muffins on the inn's porch, the sun came out, right on cue. This was convenient for our 3½ mile hike on the Pemi Trail. The path ran along the Pemigewasset River, crossing its narrower width several times. As a bonus, it seemed to be occupied by no one but us.

We took our time, stopping for pictures in meadows, and in the sparse forest where the sun poked through the hardwoods. These were the types of woods that classic fairy tales favored for their settings. Like the childhood tales, one could picture the forces of light and darkness fighting it out in this speckled northern jungle. I think I was born a tree-hugger.

When our hike was over, it was time to pay our respects to the Old Man of the Mountain memorial. At this point, I must digress to explain the significance of the Old Man. For generations of New Hampshire residents, the Old Man symbolized the state's strength, solidity, and probably stubbornness. The Old Man himself was actually a rock formation whose profile looked like that of, you guessed it, an old man, complete with forehead, eye, nose, and chin. For somewhere between thousands and millions of years it looked out over the western edge of the White Mountains. In 1945, New Hampshire proudly and affectionately adopted it as the state symbol, harboring an emotional attachment to it that baffles the outsider.

Tragically for its many devotees, the Old Man of the Mountain collapsed in May of 2003. Official records of the event state that there were no casualties, but New Hampshirites will quickly point out, sadly, that there was one very large granite fatality. The profile beloved and anthropomorphized by so many was gone but far from forgotten. In fact, at press time, the online scrapbook of memorials to the Old Man runs ninety-three pages long.[*]

Following the unfortunate occurrence, two debates began. The first was whether or not to attempt to rebuild the profile. Thousands of emails, letters, and blogs weighed in on both sides of the issue. In the end, largely due to an unstable geologic structure, it was decided that the rock should be left as is. In

---

[*] see www.nhstateparks.org/uploads/pdf/OldManScrapbook.pdf

order to memorialize the Old Man, however, the state park has installed a few posts that help the viewer replicate the experience of seeing the Old Man as he once was. Each post is about six feet tall, with a carefully calculated miniature of the profile attached to the top. When the viewer stands behind it, his line of sight is situated so that the model profile fits exactly onto the backdrop of the mountain, creating the illusion that the Old Man is alive and well, (or at least as alive as a rock formation can reasonably be).

The other debate is one that, thankfully, has not come to the public's attention, or else we would surely be permanently banned from the state of New Hampshire. Given the date of the collapse, and given our track record of large scale destruction in places where we plan to take or have recently taken trips, I feel that Senator and I may be to blame. On our first out-of-state adventure together, we traveled through six states, including New Hampshire.[*] While the trip took place in August of 2003, it was in May of 2003 that I blurted out a half-serious invitation to Senator, asking him to join me on a road trip to New England. Knowing us, it was probably uttered just moments before the Old Man fell. Still, since we had not actually planned the trip at that point, we may be absolved on a technicality. Geez, I hope they never find out...

After visiting the Old Man's final resting place, we drove to The Basin. Here pools of shallow swirling water ran across smooth rocks. It was a great spot to take a break, have a snack, or just cool your feet in the icy water. A short path led to a waterfall with more whirlpools. Lying in the center of one pool was a sort of L-shaped rock that the natives have dubbed "The Old Man's Foot", but we definitely can't be blamed for that loss.

Seeking out waterfalls can be addicting, so we drove on to another spot that our inn's host had suggested. Sabbaday Falls

---

[*] Shameless plug: see *How to Read a Compass in the Dark*

rewards anyone willing to walk less than half a mile with several distinct levels of an increasingly swiftly moving waterfall. Each tier is unique. The top is relatively calm, but the rock is positioned so that it swirls and hits the next level with enough force to make a large, lapping splash. Just as it gets comfortable with that cadence, it slips into a very narrow notch. The constrained space builds up even more pressure, creating a deep, narrow trough below. Amazingly, at every point along the four-story cascade, the water is clear.

Supposedly these falls were named Sabbaday because workers here had once laid down their tools in honor of the sabbath. Understandably, given its tranquil and relaxing atmosphere, the legend has no record of the workers picking their tools back up. I can't say I would, either. Some places were created for pure enjoyment.*

We left Sabbaday Falls and drove back toward the town. Vegetarian dining options were a little on the scarce side, so we went back to the same place we had eaten the night before. Reprised Mexican fare on a patio with an incredible view sounded just fine to us. Our server looked at us strangely, then smiled. She must have remembered that we had tipped her well.

The sun was quickly slipping behind the mountains, which meant only one thing. It was time for the Great Moose Stakeout, Take 2. Again we drove to the rumored hot spot for moose nightlife. Again we were deprived of any moose sightings. Senator buckled his seatbelt. "You know what would really suck?" he asked.

"If we came all the way here and never saw a moose?" I ventured.

"If the moose was right behind us the whole time." I quickly turned around, half expecting to catch a glimpse of a

---

* Whereas, in Illinois, the tale most likely would have been attributed to some union contract violation and resulting labor dispute.

giggling Bullwinkle ducking back into the woods, but there was nothing. We gave up and started back down The Kanc.

A few miles down the road we could see two cars pulled over. "Now here we've got something!" Senator announced as he pulled the car over. I strained my eyes to see if anything was at the edge of the woods. Sure enough, a small adult moose was leisurely nibbling by the side of the road. He seemed pretty uninterested in his viewing public, barely looking up. I suppose this was a good thing, but it did not allow us to get a good picture. I smiled in satisfaction anyway. We had finally seen our real live moose.

Back at our room we had time to relax before going to bed. Senator browsed the weather forecast on t.v. While I leafed through a chapter of a book written by a local storyteller. In the background I could hear the predictions for some rain during the night. It didn't sound like it would interfere with anything during the daytime hours, so I dismissed it. After an hour or so of British sitcom reruns, we snuggled in for a good rest, taking advantage of a cool northern breeze.

It was only about 10:30pm, but we were already falling asleep, probably due to so much hiking and fresh air. I mumbled that I thought I could hear motorcycles in the distance, perhaps coming down the highway. The noise continued to roll along, but the bikers never approached. Senator then realized that it was thunder. Again the mountains were magnifying sounds with their echoes.

For a while it was relaxing, but we soon had to close the window. The wind had picked up considerably, and the lightning was flashing almost nonstop. Still the thunder bounced around the valley. We fell asleep to quite a show.

And then, BLAM! I jumped up and grabbed Senator, yelling for him as a white flash temporarily blinded me. In the split second before I could assess my surroundings, I thought a bomb had gone off. My heart was pounding and I thought we had to escape. Between being awoken from a dead sleep, sleeping in a strange room, and hearing one of the loudest crashes I have ever heard, I was terrified.

Then everything was black, and a little bit quieter. By the time Senator understood what was happening, I figured out that lightning had blown up a transformer. We were without power, but no real harm was done. Well, it was official. Senator and Wendy V had arrived in the White Mountains.

*   *   *

It was a fitful night for me, and, consequently, for Senator. We were up early, exhausted, but glad to see that the power had been restored. As we stumbled through our morning routine, I listened to the weatherman beam out his prediction for a gorgeous day. The sky outside wasn't convinced by his optimism yet, but we packed our necessities and got into our car anyway. We had a train to catch.

Once again we drove The Kanc. This time we rode the entire length, watching the clouds gradually break up overhead. By the time we reached North Conway, the sun was out in full force. The bustling train station gave no hint of the strong storms that had swept through the area during the night.

As we stood in line to board the train for a five hour round trip excursion, it occurred to me that we had never ridden a train together.* In celebration of the event, we headed for the open air car once we were aboard. Instead of rows of seats, long benches faced the large glassless window openings, providing the ultimate in widescreen viewing. This was the highlight of the trip, and I had been imagining it for months. I felt sorry for the poor saps in first class; they had to stick to their enclosed

---

* Unless you count the commuter line into Chicago, or the New York subway. These, however, are not known for their proximity to natural beauty. And by 'natural beauty', I don't mean some homeless guy flashing you.

assigned seats. We could roam freely from bench to bench, taking in every glimpse of scenery.

For the next two hours we rode the rails, gliding through forests, over rocky river beds, and around mountains. Lush masses of ferns carpeted the ground beneath most of the trees. Occasionally the train passed a waterfall, and we strained our necks to see its top. At the beginning of the ride there was narration, but the guide wisely wrapped it up, letting the scenery speak for itself.

Twice we crept our way across bridges. One of them was ominously named Frankenstein Trestle. At eighty and ninety feet, theses bridges were not for the faint of heart, but we enjoyed every minute of it. Why worry about a train on a bridge when you've been in a plane in the sky and a boat on the ocean?

I also made another pleasant observation. People still wave to trains. Something about an engine plugging along, steadfastly pulling its chain of cars, brings a smile to people's faces. Perhaps it is a romantic appreciation for a form of transportation that played a major role in the development of this great nation. Perhaps it is the most interesting thing going on in small towns. Whatever the reason, old and young waved us by as though we were all celebrities.

I did not realize how far we had climbed in elevation until we reached the train station at the other end. Looking over the valley we could see the pencil line of our tracks far beneath. We got out and stretched our legs, much closer to the clouds than when we had left. It was a little foggy, but it only added to the serenity. This was my kind of layover.

We passed the next hour walking near a mountain pond and reading the stories of the region's early inhabitants. In one case, in order to get the family's four children to school, the children had to take the train to town. For physical reasons, the train was not able to stop by their home. The engineer could, however, slow the train down enough for a man to swing out and grab each child, who had readied himself/herself by looping his/her arm around to form a hook. I would have loved to have seen that!

The ride back went quickly. Passengers moved around the car trying to determine the best view, which was not easy with so much to see. At one point, most if not all of us were looking to the right. Senator happened to be looking the other way, just in time to catch a glimpse of a black bear cub. It was the first time he had seen one in the wild.

Soon we were pulling back into the station. We slowed down to a few miles per hour, passing some old, dilapidated caboose cars that looked like they had many great stories to tell. Finally the train came to a stop. Stepping onto the platform and seeing the busy town made it seem like we had quietly sneaked away to some fantasy land. I can only sum it up by saying that roads take us to where we are supposed to go. Rails take us to where we are supposed to *be*.

As we started to leave the station, I remembered that one of the attendants had mentioned that a freight house was open. We walked up the ramp of the simple, unmarked building to the side door. There, in the approximate space of a large living room, was an elaborate model railroad. We had stumbled onto the 500 square foot layout of the North Conway Model Railroad Club.

I have been fascinated by miniatures of all types ever since I fell in love with the dollhouse that my parents designed, built, and decorated for me when I was five. Senator was intrigued, too. The more we looked, the more the carefully created landscape revealed itself. We counted at least seven trains operating simultaneously. They sped around curves, through tunnels, and among all of the typical buildings that a late 1940s town would possess. At one point the backdrop melted into a wharf, complete with a plane flying overhead. In deference to its New Hampshire heritage, the layout also featured a logging mill, as well as a car-moose accident by the side of one of its roads.

I could have stared, mesmerized, for hours, but we were both hungry, so we searched for the Indian restaurant we had passed on our way into town. Arriving twenty minutes before they opened meant we were taunted by the spicy aromas until they unlocked the doors for us. A kind older lady brought us water and took our order. We ordered plenty and we ate plenty. It's truly amazing what some cultures can do with potatoes, peas, and cauliflower! As we finished the last of our garlic naan, I declared it one of our best dates of the past nine years. Now if I could only learn to make an authentic curry...

* * *

It was a little sad to leave the White Mountains the next morning; everything had felt so right the entire time we were there. Still, I was anxious to see the Lakes Region of New Hampshire. At breakfast that morning, as we thanked our hosts for a wonderful stay, we were advised to take a short hike on Rattlesnake Mountain. It sounded lovely, provided the rattlesnake part of the name was a misnomer.

We traveled south on Route 3, making light mental note of which towns looked inviting and livable (just in case). When we reached the parking lot for the trailhead, it was packed, but Senator squeezed us into the last available spot. I had already grown so accustomed to the solitude on most of the trails that I mildly dreaded seeing other hikers. Hopefully the view would be worth it.

As it turned out, the trail was busy, but it was great to see people of all ages enjoying it. Instead of parking their butts in front of televisions or video games, there were kids actually breathing fresh air and panting their way up the rugged path. At the other end of the spectrum, we regularly passed very capable elderly ladies plodding up the hill with their walking sticks. It was an unusual site, at least for someone from the Midwest. I jokingly called it the Menopause Trail, until I learned that the ladies were part of a group with an even better name—The Over the Hill Hiking Club, of course!

At the top, the view of Squam Lake was stunning. A 180° expanse revealed dense trees on many islands that interrupted the intensely blue water. This was where the movie *On Golden Pond* was filmed, which I later learned is quite popular with the over sixty female crowd. Ah, it all made sense now. We nodded our 'good afternoon' to the groups of seniors enjoying their picnic lunches on the rocks above the lake. I admired them, and I hope we will be doing the same thing when we are their age.

I checked the time as we bounced back down the trail to the parking lot. We had plenty of time to drive to Weirs Beach for the last great adventure of the trip-- the Sophie C. mailboat. I don't recall how I originally learned that there existed such a thing as a floating post office. I suppose it must have been a blurb in a guidebook, or a feature on a related travel website, but it sounded like a unique opportunity, so we decided to go for it.

Weirs Beach, home of the dock for the Sophie C., as well as myriad fried food vendors and outdated gamerooms, was the type of tourist trap more suited to the Wisconsin Dells than beautiful Lake Winnipesaukee[*]. Senator made at least four passes down the only street with parking before finding a spot. We dutifully deposited a few quarters in the ancient parking meter and walked toward the pavilion. Our hands were intertwined, partly in affection, and partly in apprehension as we eyed the loud chaos of families running toward the ice cream stand, the water park, and who knows where else. The serenity of the mountains beckoned us back. We silently agreed that this would be our last trip to Weird Beach, as I had now dubbed it.

Senator kissed me, then broke off for a quick pit stop. Meanwhile, I stepped up to the booth to purchase our boat

---

[*] That's Algonquian for "My mommy and daddy inherited a trust fund and all I got was this crummy island!"

tickets. In front of me was a mom with an obnoxious child. She dug through her purse for funds while trying, unsuccessfully, to pacify the brat hanging from her leg. I whispered a prayer of thanks for the miracle of contraception. After what seemed like an hour, but was more likely five minutes, she finished her transaction and left.

I approached the booth and the attendant, determined not to spend another minute of my vacation around unruly children. "Hello," I began. "Do you sell tickets for the 2:00 mailboat run?"

"Yes, it boards right here at 1:30," answered the attendant politely.

"Great. I have one more question. Does that tour attract many kids?" I inquired, not even vaguely trying to hide my disdain for her previous customer.

"Oh, no! It's very rare that children go on that one," she reassured. To her everlasting credit in the field of customer service, she had caught my drift completely.

"Thank you very much! I'll take two..."

Senator returned as I was signing the credit slip, and we walked down the ramp to our boat's dock. We soon boarded for two hours of sunny, breezy cruising. The boat is actually a valid branch of the United State Post Office-- albeit a floating branch-- that delivers and retrieves mail for five islands during the warm months. For a modest fee passengers can ride along, venturing into the cabin to mail items or purchase stamps if necessary.

As we left the shore, we nestled back in our seats to appreciate the fresh air above one of the world's cleanest bodies of water. Despite year-round usage, Lake Winnipesaukee remains crystal clear. We learned that this is because of its unique geography. The lake is completely spring fed by runoff mountain water. Then the water drains into a river, acting as a giant filtration system.

In between enjoying the ride and the occasional spray when hitting a wake, we stopped for the postal exchanges. At the first island, a camp of young boys and girls ran out to meet the boat, eager for letters from home, and to buy ice cream treats from the captain. At other stops families met us, some of whom brought packages to mail. Others just waved, happy to see a glimpse of the mainlanders... (as long as it was only a glimpse). At our final stop, two well-rehearsed sisters worked in tandem to grab the mail bag and pass off their outgoing items.

Everyone was so friendly and excited to greet the boat. For two hours it was as though no technological means of communication existed. While some islands have been more modernized, many still rely on the fading art of letter writing to patiently give and receive news. Swimming instead of texting? Sitting around a campfire instead of a television? What concepts.

As the Sophie C. pulled into port, I subconsciously felt around my bag for my car keys. We both wanted to make a beeline from the boat to our vehicle, bypassing all of the crazy boardwalk amusements. The mailboat experience had been wonderful, but once we were on land, we couldn't get out of town fast enough. It was only a twenty minutes' drive to the inn where we would be staying, and we were ready for a quiet evening. It was time to begin the slow, steady process of leaving Vacationworld and coming back to Realworld.

* * *

When we arrived at the Ballard House Inn, we were greeted by Brian and Newton. Brian, we would soon learn, had a knack for blending mile-a-minute energetic enthusiasm with a laid back style of hospitality. He immediately treated us like family, showing us all around the 1790 home. It was open, airy, and beautifully updated in such a way as to preserve its historical integrity without being fussy. I hated the thought of leaving New Hampshire for the Midwest, but I could tell this would be a great place to spend our last night there.

No, I didn't forget about Newton. Newton is enormous and silent and a dog, perhaps a collie. I don't really know my breeds, but whatever his pedigree, I could have ridden him around the ten acres of the home's property. He sniffed us once or twice, gave a casual wave of his tail, and escorted us to the bottom of the stairs, possibly indicating that our room was on the second floor.

Inside the room I flopped on the bed and stared out the window. We overlooked a lake that was perfectly framed by hardwood treetops. Brian explained that the view was obstructed when he purchased the property only months before, so he took it upon himself to employ a chainsaw. Voila! Million-dollar view. He was also proud to point out that he didn't need permits or red tape to do so.

As Senator napped, I turned the television on low, searching for a weather forecast. Instead, I got sucked into an NHPTV[*] special about Granny D., aka Doris Haddock. Fed up with political campaign corruption, this spunky New Hampshire senior decided to promote reform by taking a long walk-- from California to Washington D.C., in fact. After all, she was only eighty-nine years old! All along the trail, well-wishers greeted her, joined her, and encouraged her. She didn't solve all of the problems of our political system, but she did gain positive attention from both Democrat and Republican representatives, aiding in the eventual passing of the McCain/Feingold bill to remove unregulated 'soft' money from campaigns.[†] I love these people.

*   *   *

Thursday morning was our last in New England. By my calculation, we would not be able to return for at least another twenty-one months, but who was counting? That's right; I was. We had plenty of time to get home, so we enjoyed a leisurely and chatty breakfast next to the original colonial hearth in the dining

---

[*] New Hampshire Public Television

[†] For more on Granny D., visit grannyd.com.

room. Our ulterior motive in engaging our friendly host in conversation was, of course, to pump him for information.

Was he from here originally? No, he made the big move when his Pittsburgh construction company dipped during the recession. Best decision they've ever made.

"They?" Yep. Ironically, his wife was in Chicago on business that very weekend. She had called the previous night from a hot, humid hotel that had lost power to say that she had just put in her two-weeks' notice. She would be retired and a full time New Hampshirite in fourteen days.

How serious are locals about the whole 'Live Free or Die' thing? Very. Come up, do your thing, don't bother anyone else, and no one will bother you.

Brian kept offering up information, and Newton wasn't hurrying away from his claimed spot at Senator's feet, so I pressed further. What about the property taxes? Every time an outsider brings up the fact that it must be marvelous not to pay any state income tax, native New Hampshirites counter with a well-rehearsed lament about how high their property taxes are. Brian laughed at this. When he quoted us his actual numbers, we laughed, too. For a three-story historical inn and ten forested acres that ran up to a lake, he paid roughy twice what we pay for a two bedroom ranch on less than a ¼ acre. I believe I may have been misty eyed...

Eventually we could linger no longer, so we checked out, said our good-byes, patted Newton, and somewhat awkwardly participated in the impromptu bear hug from Brian. It was great to meet someone who so truly appreciated his home and his life. Good for him. Good for his wife too, whom I imagined as throwing her high heels in the trash just before boarding a plane out of Midway. And good for Newton.

We were on our way home, too. Hours were passed driving and remembering mannerisms and anecdotes of the people we had met during the last week. What characters. All too soon we were out of New England. After a long stretch in New York, we passed the halfway point, continuing southwest along Lake Erie.

I was making the transition back to the Midwest gradually, and not exactly willingly. Of course, it's always good to get back to one's own bed and bathroom, but I felt like I had been very far away for a very long time. The adjustment was strange. Senator was more optimistic, looking forward to the many upcoming activities in the remainder of 2012. If I consider it all honestly though, the truth is that I would rather live anywhere with him than in New England without him. (Just don't tell him I said that.)

Anywhere, that is, except maybe Cleveland. No, I'm not just rehashing tired stereotypes, pinning the Ohio city as the proverbial "mistake by the lake", but its hotels certainly did nothing to promote the city's good points. We were getting very tired, and we figured that in an urban area it would be easy to find a clean, reasonably comfortable hotel. Exit after exit frustrated us. Either there was a severe shortage of lodging, or what was available was unacceptable at best. The supply-demand ratio apparently allowed low-quality establishments to charge an arm and a leg, when all they really deserved was a certain central finger.

My point is best illustrated by the Days Inn we happened upon. We pulled into the lot, noting that the posted nightly rate could not be justified for any room a building like that could contain. Senator shut off the car and we climbed out, hoping it would be the last stop for the night. The small and stinky lobby was not promising. "Do you have any *non*smoking rooms available?" I ventured, remembering that some states still allow indoor smoking.

"Yeah."

"We'd like to see one," I stated flatly. The obese, sloppy desk attendant shrugged at her fellow employee and handed us the key, telling us the room number. We thanked her and went upstairs, already 90% sure we would not be staying. I couldn't help but notice that the second floor was equally aromatic to the first.

When we opened the door, no words were needed. We simultaneously fell into hysterical laughter. The bed was unmade, with mangled sheets and pillows strewn about. Of course. So this was the 'sample' room to convince us to patronize the joint, huh?

I don't think either of us was able to choke down our laughter enough to talk until we reached the front desk again. "Here," I said, handing the woman the key. "We'll pass," I added, through more tears of laughter. She looked puzzled.

"The bed wasn't even made!" Senator sputtered out. "It's the most basic part of the room!" The woman started to apologize, but we were already leaving, still laughing too hard to be angry.

Eventually we did find tolerable accommodations, but home now sounded better than ever. We spent our last day of the trip driving at the pace of the homeward bound. (It was my job to watch for cops.) We found none, and happily, none found us. There's always next year...

Chapter 4
Piece of Cake:
Late May 2013

Just when I thought this book was done... By August of 2012, I was back to a new school year, and Senator had returned to serving on the front lines of the retail industry, wringing forty hours out of each week amid regular trips to Chicago to record live concerts or play keyboards for the band Death and Memphis.* Concurrently, there was more mixing taking place in my basement than on the top five Food Network shows combined. Thus, as is the routine every fall, I had resigned myself to several months on traveling suspension. There were, of course, a few trips within the tri-state area for music purposes, but nothing that involved a good hike or stunning scenery.

We also took what precious little free time we had together for minor adventures on the home front. When the misery of one of the hottest summers on record had subsided, we brought out the bicycles for one last hurrah. Autumn was upon us, and my favorite months beckoned. We even discovered a

---

* Our friend Anthony later suggested the name Death and Taxes, which we found preferable-- especially given the fact that the band was entirely from Illinois, with no known Tennessee connections-- but the name was not Senator's choice.

nearby apple orchard.*

It was during the 24-hour period following one of these trips to the apple orchard that the fever-pitched pace of our lives turned a corner. We were walking around, hand-in-hand, casually discussing future plans and financial goals. We both agreed on the general outline of the plan, specifically how long Senator would work at the bookstore, but this aspect somehow did not feel accurate. I shook my head calmly and submitted my prediction. "I don't mean to sound negative, and of course I want everything to work out, but I just don't see that store staying open another ten years..." He nodded vaguely, and we started to select our apples.

The next morning we both left for work. As was my habit, I checked my email at lunch, in case Senator had been able to sneak a quick note to me. Usually I would find nothing awaiting me if he was on a day shift, so I was pleasantly surprised when his name popped up in my inbox. When I read his email, I was even more surprised. He briefly informed me of what he had learned in his weekly managers' meeting. In about four months the store would close down permanently, and he would be laid off. Wow. Score one for my prophetic gut feeling.

---

* Apple Jacks is "Open Daily-noon". Upon further inquiry, one discovers that these seemingly ample hours include the following stipulations:

1. There must be more than two people around to bother unlocking the entrance gate. Anything less is a waste of the farmer's time. Furthermore, at least one of the vehicles waiting to come in must be a pickup truck, preferably American-made, (although some exceptions may be granted in the high harvest season).

2. Noon is not necessarily the same as 12:00. This particularly applies on Sundays, if the preacher is on a roll and fails to notice the increasingly fidgety congregation, thereby letting church out late.

3. If you have to ask about a closing time, you obviously weren't there on time.

Of course, the evening's conversation centered around alternate plans and ideas regarding our budget's future. Strangely though, from the first moment I learned of the impending job loss, I had nothing but positive-- and even excited-- anticipation about it. Contrary to my nature, it just felt completely correct. And why not? If one gut feeling could be so accurate, couldn't two? I knew in my heart it was going to be for the best.

Senator was not as convinced, which spoke of his strong work ethic and sense of responsibility. Still, he started to daydream with me about the advantages this meant for our two-person family. Weekends off together-- what a concept! No more corporate bullshit! Proper amounts of time to devote to music and maybe even books! Sleep! By the time his last day rolled around, he was both ready and relieved to go. Yet on his first day 'off', it became apparent that he would be as busy as ever. The following four months were a blur, documenting more sets of live music than ever before.[*]

As it turned out, that spring and the previous fall had been busy for my sister, too. In September, I received a very long and excited email, in which she gave me the scoop on the guy she was dating. Her elation spilled off the screen. After a few past conversations urging her away from other guys whom I thought would eventually bring her grief, I was so happy that she had found someone who treated her so well. I predicted that they would be married by summer. My brother laughed at me, but by December my sister was engaged and had decided on a late-May wedding. I should have made my brother put some money on that one.

Not being hindered by a retail schedule, Senator was free for the Memorial Day wedding. My school had just enough of a

---

[*] At press time, Senator has recorded musicians from five different continents and about a dozen different countries.

break between spring and summer semesters that I could attend, too. We would need a few days, since the wedding would take place in Missouri, about seven hours from us. Finally everything was set for us to witness Heidi and Philip's big event.

A few weeks before the wedding, my youngest brother called to consult Senator. The two of them would be in charge of setting up some sound equipment for the outdoor ceremony. They are both hard workers and know their stuff, so they agreed to meet at the site of the wedding/reception the day before the wedding. Since I was not involved in the ceremony itself, I offered my services as a budding assistant technician as well. They had a good plan in place, and it all seemed relatively routine.

Soon the morning of the rehearsal arrived. We left town early and had an easy trip into Missouri, despite their infamously bad highway drivers. After checking into our hotel and relaxing a bit, we left for the refinished barn that Heidi had booked for the reception. Weather permitting, the ceremony would be held outside on the same grounds.

Thus, the madness began. The barn should have been simple to find, at least, according to the map I had. As it turned out however, the appropriate numbered road sign was nowhere to be found. We tried several roads that seemed to be possible options, but we turned back each time. Eventually we parked the car and gave up. So I did what all practical American adults do when hopelessly befuddled; I called my mommy. "Do you have *any* idea where in the world this place is?" I pleaded.

My mother was in a car with one of the bridesmaids. My dad was in a different vehicle with another driver. It's not that they wouldn't have liked to be together on this, their daughter's wedding eve. Their van, which was packed to the ceiling with equipment and supplies, had chosen a most inconvenient time to breakdown. It sat idle at Heidi's house. After an all-out scramble to repack all necessary items, they had divided up to squeeze in where they could fit.

Shockingly, Mom had no idea where the place was either. According to the GPS of the girl with whom she was riding, either the road did not exist, or as they say in the rural countries, "Ya' cain't get there from here." Collectively, we decided to turn down a sparse gravel road. It did not seem possible that a sizable venue could be down such a deserted road, but we tried it anyway. After winding for a while, we crept over a wooden bridge and turned a corner to see the barn in full view. I wondered how that bridge, which sat so low, would have fared during our floods that had been occurring regularly in northern Illinois that spring.

We parked the cars in the gravel side lot. It only held about a dozen cars, so I guessed that guests would have to park along the road, but that wasn't my problem. I was just the Sound Guy's Helper. Senator and I got out of our car and looked for my brother.

Caleb was busy unpacking sound equipment, and unpacking sound equipment, and unpacking sound equipment. Based on what I had envisioned, I was expecting a microphone or two, a stand, some cable, and maybe a p.a. speaker. This was to be a far more elaborate production, complicated by the fact that the barn provided nothing in the way of audio, video, or electrical support. With the exception of a faithful 4-foot ladder, all items had been borrowed from Caleb's church and imported south.

Once the lights, fixtures, speakers, cables, video projectors, microphone, computers, and even sound board had been loaded in, the three of us went to work. Operating from the standpoint of a dedicated pessimist, I always allow plenty of time for setup in any situation, naturally assuming that mild disasters will delay start times. This night was no different, but the hour and a half or so that I had (generously) figured on turned into four hours of the three of us hurrying to finish.

Meanwhile, my family and Heidi's friends worked to arrange and decorate the barn. Somewhere in the middle of it all, they squeezed in a rehearsal as well. Had we not all had such determined personalities, we would still be setting up.

Eventually we had to call it a night. Exhausted and hungry, we caravanned to Lambert's Restaurant, arriving just before they stopped seating people.* Dinner was good, the flying rolls did not disappoint, and my sister and her fiancé were giddier than ever thinking about their dream wedding. The rest of my family was mentally strategizing for the next day's car repairs, ceremony, and reception. It seemed like we had all worked so hard, and yet there was still so much left to be done. As we drove back to the hotel, my mom voiced a self-reminder to check on the toilet paper situation. "Huh?"

"Yeah, I noticed that there was only one roll of paper in the only bathroom in the place," she explained in a voice that revealed her dwindling energy. "And I also need to pick up coffee creamer. About two bottles."

"Okay," I said flatly, wondering if it was typical for the mother-of-the-bride to have to add an extra two plies to her concerns.

*   *   *

On the day of the wedding, we actually had no early commitments. Though Senator had offered to help, he was told that there was really nothing he could do to assist with Operation Van Startup. My brothers would take my dad back to Heidi's, where his van had last functioned. The three of them would work on it and either 1.)get it running, allowing my parents to happily drive to the wedding and then home the next day, or 2.)run out of time, parts, or patience, necessitating more carpool shuffling, and possibly stranding my parents in Missourah.

---

*   Home of the 'throwed rolls'!

84

Our plan was to rest up, have a bite, go for a short swim, and get ready. Rendezvous time was 12:30pm at the barn. So why then, was this biologically programmed night person staring at the hotel ceiling at 6:30am? I had popped my eyes open in response to my mom's comment the night before. Seriously? She should have been getting pampered and smiling for photographs instead of worrying about how 200-some people were going to cream their coffees and wipe their asses.

Senator lay on his side, asleep. I got out of bed and threw on some clothes. In my mind I retraced the route to a Walmart we had passed the night before. I raided my purse for license, phone, and cash. By the time I came out of a momentary pit stop in the bathroom, Senator was getting ready as well. "I'm sorry. I didn't want to wake you. I'm just going on a creamer-and-toilet-paper quest. You can sleep. I know my way and I'll be back in just--"

"Like heck!" he interrupted. "You aren't going around all these hillbillies alone!" Though I was less convinced of an imminent early morning southern uprising in the dairy aisle of Walmart, I was touched by his concern.

"Okay, c'mon," I agreed, realizing there was no point in arguing. Ten minutes later I was scouting a suitable 12-pack... of Northern.

By the time we got back to the hotel, it was clear that we were done sleeping. Adrenaline had kicked in, and it was going to be a long day. Senator and I deposited our goods in our room and headed for the hotel's breakfast room. Pouring ourselves coffee and stacking a few plates with fruit, eggs, and muffins, we found an out-of-the-way table to contemplate our roles. Senator would be Caleb's partner in running sound outside during the ceremony and inside during the reception. I would manage drinks and cakes, and generally assist my parents as necessary. Again, it sounded simple on the surface.

As we finished our coffee, we saw my parents enter the

room. They were smiling, and my dad was joking, so that was a good sign. Behind them my brothers followed. The mood was optimistic, and Dad was fairly confident that he could get the van running. The man always amazes me when it comes to tackling frustrating projects.

We visited for a short while and agreed to meet at the barn in three hours. "Oh yeah. By the way. We picked up creamer. And toilet paper... just in case..." I casually mentioned. My mom thanked us with gratitude that surpassed the deed, and with that, we left to change for the pool.

Like most hotel pools, a few boys in the 7-11-year old bracket reigned over the waters. Their two (presumably) mothers began doling out the rules as we approached. "Now Michael, make sure you don't splash anyone!" I smiled in acknowledgment of her consideration, but I also thought how silly it was for anyone to expect to stay dry while swimming.

"Austin, don't hold your brother's head under water! I mean it!" No she didn't. Senator and I tucked our toes into the water, which we judged to be roughly the temperature of newly melted ice cream. Naturally Michael, Austin, and Austin's now-pouting little brother were not at all fazed by the frigid pool. We opted to sit on the sidelines-- as far away as possible from the cackling, nagging mothers. "Stop that right now! You're going to get a time out! I'm serious!" No she wasn't.

The blanket of humidity was thick. After twenty minutes or so of watching Senator almost fall asleep under it, and the clouds almost sprout a shower above it, I was ready to go in. Just then Michael made a break for the exercise room. "Get out of there! I think that's just for grown-ups. You're going to get into big trouble!" No he wasn't.

As we got ready, Senator asked about the food plan. I had sort of forgotten about that part. It was almost noon, and no one would be eating until at least 8:00pm. Even then it would be mainly finger foods. "Everyone's going to be starving. When will your parents eat?" I didn't have a good answer to his question. It wasn't like anyone could just duck out for a quick snack once we were working at the barn. It was a good half hour ride from anything other than more barns. He then suggested yet another Walmart excursion. "We can pick up a cheap cooler and some ice. There's a Subway inside, so we can get a bunch of sandwiches." It was by far the best solution.

So back to Walmart we went-- this time formal. As time was of the essence, we decided to divide and conquer. Senator went in search of a cooler and ice, while I got in line at Subway. I am infamous for taking far too long to choose food for just myself, let alone an entire family. I said a quick prayer for guidance[*], and shrugged my slipping sheer scarf back over my long gown. Oh yeah, and I was still wearing my driving sunglasses. I must have looked like Springfield's excuse for a has-been B movie star.

As I looked up from my minor wardrobe adjustment, a soft light fell upon the suspended menu, illuminating the perfect sandwich options for each member of my family-- the vegetarians, the meatarians, and the omnivores. *Hallelujah!* I rattled off toppings and condiments, careful to keep pace with the Sandwich Artist[†], so as not to slow down the line. Just as the last foot-long was being wrapped up, Senator appeared with his scavenger hunt items. "Is a styrofoam cooler alright?" he asked. "It looks like we're going fishing."

"A styrofoam cooler is absolutely perfect!" I laughed.

The cashier smiled at us. "Are you guys going on a picnic today?"

"Nope, working at a wedding," I replied. He looked confused, but politely wished us a good time. I can only imagine

---

[*] If He feeds the sparrows and dresses the lilies, I was banking on the fact that He would have a spare minute to show me what to order.

[†] Not my term; blame Subway.

what he told his coworkers about us.

After about twenty minutes, we came to the elusive turn that led to the barn. This time we weren't going to miss it. As we hung a right, I happened to look down toward the ground. There, standing a grandiose two feet off the ground, half buried by weeds, was a sign for the place. *Well that was useful. No wonder we all missed it.*

It should have been my first clue. While the barn itself was lovely, no accommodations were made to suggest that it was a reception venue. In addition to the nonexistent parking lot, not a foot of ground had been paved. Good luck if you happen to be wearing high heels or rolling in via wheelchair. The excessive dust and gravel made me feel much better about not washing my car before leaving home. It now looked like an upgraded Hudson for the Joads.

We stepped inside to a flurry of activity. Bridesmaids were still running around decorating tables. My mom was working on the head table. Empty and half-empty cardboard boxes lay strewn about from their original pile.[*] The bride and groom were making last minute decisions about specifics. Outside, my dad, (who had spent his morning fixing the van,)[†] was attempting to arrange the seating in a suitable and bride-approved fashion. My brother Caleb was hard at work organizing further sound logistics, and my brother Jason was looking for a place to change into his groomsman gear. "Well, I guess I'll see you later..." Senator said. I nodded, realizing we would both be busy for the next twelve hours or so. We kissed and split up to assist the 'rents.

I calculated about six hours until showtime and about ten

---

[*] I later learned what a massive mound of STUFF my parents had packed, transported, unpacked, repacked, unpacked, repacked, and tranported back to their home. It ranged from kitchen supplies to decorations, to beverage servers, to lanterns and beyond.

[†] Again, *hallelujah!*

hours worth of work left. No problem. It was a little overwhelming, but I had confidence in my Essential Other and in my family. I walked toward my mom, who was now wrestling a large adhesive tablecloth. If I may break into alliteration Reader, she was quite the lovely lady in her long, lavender lace. As she handed me one end of the mile of unfurling plastic, she complained that her hair had not turned out how she wanted. I waved a yard of tablecloth out of my line of vision so I could glance at her. She looked fantastic. I told her I thought it was beautiful, and I meant it.

Tablecloth threatened into submission, I peeked outside to see how my dad was doing. Prior to the day of the wedding, it was our understanding that certain hay bales, which now sat partially moldy and permanent, would be removed by the owners. We were also led to believe that chairs would be set up. The former was completely not the case. Said bales o' hay had no intention of leaving their prime spot, which overlooked the panoramic field. The latter part-- about the chairs-- was true, provided *we* set them up. This amounted to my dad and Senator stealing chairs from the reception room, dragging them outside, and positioning them. With the new knowledge that chairs were in short supply, Senator and I planned to grab them up after the ceremony and run them back inside for the reception, which would immediately follow. After four years of live recording, we had become masters of the quick set change, so we felt capable.

With the seating situation under control, I turned my attentions to food. Food-- that's right! I had forgotten that there was a styrofoam cooler full of not bait, but sub sandwiches. Senator gathered my family and insisted they take a quick meal break. I know they must have been hungry because my dad didn't even waste time refusing.

I actually was more hot than hungry, so I bypassed subs in lieu of a break to tackle some more planning. Originally, four sheet cakes were to be posted on four tables in corners of the room. While I appreciated the symmetry, this made me nervous. I had visions of rambunctious little kids running around the artful confections, pausing only to dip fingers into the tempting frosting.

Then there was the possibility of a table toppling over before I could rescue it. In a crowded reception room, there was no way I could monitor all four corners to prevent disaster. There were also the logistics of how Heidi's friend Jackie and I would serve cake from four different stations. We were good, but we had not yet perfected the art of being in two places at once.

I was relieved when Heidi announced a change in plans. Not four tables, but one—good! The only catch was that it was the same table that currently held the name placecards. If I planned my time well, though, I could snag the table as soon as all the guests were seated. They would no longer need the cards, and then we could quickly transform it into the cake table, probably without anyone even noticing. The tricky part would be keeping the cake stocked. The kitchen was in the opposite corner of the barn as the cake table. That meant that as Jackie ran low on one cake, I would have to carry the next one through the mobs of celebrants to the cake station.*

I was pretty sure we could manage this, so I went to the

---

* Those of you in my general age bracket will remember a particularly clumsy baker on *Sesame Street*. After grandly announcing the number and flavor of his tiers of perfectly decorated cakes, he proceeded to trip and fall down the stairs with them. You knew as soon as you saw him in his pristine white chefwear, carrying the mountain of pastries toward the steps, that disaster would ensue, but it never ceased to be hilarious. I laughed like an idiot as the frosting flew. Flash forward. Now I dreaded the horror of losing these cakes in a similar calamity. My mind recalled every *Three Stooges* episode involving women in long gowns and pearls flinging creamy desserts at men in suits, and vice-versa. Fun? Potentially. Part of my sister's dream wedding? Not likely.

kitchen to scope out the cakes physically. As the kitchen was roughly twice the size of my small kitchen at home, it contained only one refrigerator. Since that had to be used for hors d'oeuvres, the cakes were stacked neatly in their boxes on a large shelf in the freezer. This necessitated some executive decision making. I asked my mom when she thought I should bring each cake out of the freezer. If I did it too late, guests might be chipping into half-frozen rocks. If I did it too early, they might be drinking their cake.

Her response: "Wendy, I have no idea, but I trust you. Whatever you think you want to do, and however you want to do it, will be fine." Normally these words are very liberating to a creative person, but when you're working behind the scenes on someone else's fantasy, you don't want to be the dope to screw it up. At any rate, it was clear that Mom had no time for such details. She was onto to other projects.

I lifted one of the cakes out of the freezer, pretending I had some scientific formula that would relate its density to the time needed for thawing. For no particular reason whatsoever, I decided to take out the first cake as the guests were getting situated at their tables. That would also give me enough time to pre-cut it for ease of serving. I glanced at the small countertop next to the freezer. It was piled with trays and boxes. In one container were a few dozen delicate daisies created from hard sugar. I was told that these had to be added to each cake as well. It wasn't ideal, but I figured I could balance each cake on my knee as it hung halfway off the counter, daisy it, cut it, lift it out of its box, and carry it through the dining room.

Now it was time to help my mom with drinks. She had already set up an attractive and neat drink station. She had also started the coffee, and arranged the cream, sugar (two kinds), spoons, cups, and napkins. My primary role was Punch Queen. I would stock the large, spouted server with appropriate portions of juice and lemon-lime pop that together magically equaled punch. I would also keep the ice compartment refreshed, and the ice tea (two kinds) and water pitchers full.

For reasons unknown to me, I was looking forward to all of this. Apparently I derive profound joy from refilling liquids, or maybe it was just that the different colors looked so pretty through the clear plastic. Perhaps it was just the joy of throwing out more containers and freeing up more precious kitchen space. At any rate, I was motivated to make these beverages happen. I'd start with the easiest one first.

I took the water pitcher and went to the faucet in the kitchen, turning the right handle. Nothing came out. At this point, someone uttered a statement that will forever amaze me. "I don't think they have cold water."

"Like, at all?" I asked, certain I had misunderstood.

The owner was within earshot, and offered what she must have believed to be an acceptable solution. "You can use the faucet in the bathroom..." She should have emphasized the word 'the', as there was only one available.

Reflecting on years of waitressing, hosting others in my home, and assisting at various events involving food service, I was dumbfounded. Water is a basic feature of a kitchen. In the United States, both hot and cold are generally expected, especially when paying rental facility fees. I looked her right in the eye, half believing that the *Candid Camera* crew would reveal their hiding places at any moment. "Do you honestly mean to tell me that you don't have hot and cold running water in a *commercial* kitchen?!" She shrugged uselessly, as though I had demanded a flowing well of champagne.

"Unbelievable!" I declared, arousing Senator's attention. He came over to see what the problem was. When I explained the situation, he was even more annoyed than I was. Still, to his everlasting credit, he grabbed the pitcher and patiently waited between bathroom users to go in and tip the pitcher under the sink tap for water. Ten trips later the server was filled, with only a few strange looks from the guests coming out of the bathroom. The rest of the drink-filling went much smoother, probably because it didn't involve anything as exotic as cold water.

Beverage complications aside for the moment, Senator and I turned our attentions toward candle lighting. As western civilization has exchanged the flint and steel for the notably more practical butane lighter, this should have been an easy task. Again, we should have known better. Inside, each table had two floating tea lights that needed to be lit. Since the wicks were pressed down into the wax, they had to be removed first.

Once this was accomplished, the real fun began. The candles were nearly impossible to light while in their globes of water. On the other hand, if we lit the candles outside of the globes, there was only enough room to drop them in, along with a prayer that they did not sink, which often they did. Of course, a sunken candle is a dead candle. This turned what should have been a five minute job into a thirty minute ordeal.

With the inside finally aglow, we confidently stepped outside to light the lanterns. Though these small candles were enclosed in glass panels, the high winds challenged our ingenuity. After several failed attempts at illumination, we learned that if we tipped the top open ever so slightly, we could fit the lighter in on an angle, thereby lighting the candle and deflecting the wind. The important step here is to also remove one's scarf from the path of the flame, which thankfully, Senator reminded me to do.

After the unofficial lighting procedure, there was just enough time to get ready for the ceremony. I wasn't about to miss it because of being stuck in the kitchen. I stole a quick kiss from Senator, who was still busy with Caleb. Then I grabbed our camera and escorted myself to the second row, bride's side[*], careful not to trip on the crooked hunk of wood that served as a step to the outside.

It was the first time during the past two days that my mom looked relaxed. I noticed that her hair still looked great. My brother Jason walked down the aisle with one of the bridesmaids, glad his end of the deal was mostly complete. Soon my dad and my sister appeared, both beaming and looking incredible. Ironically, my sister suddenly looked very much like a woman to me, while my parents seemed to have grown another ten years younger since the ceremony began. I focused and snapped away, capturing my sister's bliss as well as two dimensions could. The rest of the ceremony followed the usual traditions, closing with my sister kissing her Prince Philip and becoming Mrs. Heidi Neighbour[†].

Following the ceremony, the bridal party and family were commandeered for photos. This made Senator, Jason, and I a little nervous, as we were supposed to be hustling chairs inside. Realizing the time crunch, several kind guests grabbed seats and brought them in, freeing us up for a few moments. We posed, smiled, smiled, posed, and then darted toward the barn to man (and woman) our stations.

As I was about to go through the door, I saw some commotion near my parents and the newly married couple. Just as the beautiful bride was grinning for a few final shots, a dastardly wasp had stung her under her arm. Oh no! I went to see if she was okay, simultaneously wondering where on Earth the nearest hospital was in case she had any latent sting allergies. If you knew my sister though, you would not be surprised to

---

[*] Useful tip: when attending a wedding, if you are asked which 'side' you desire, always select the bride's side, even if you only know the groom. You will have a much better view of the dress, because let's face it, if you've seen one tux, you've seen 'em all.

[†] Or as we have jokingly taken to calling her, "H'di Neighbour!"

find that she was laughing it all off. "Of *course* a wasp would sting me!" she giggled. It must have been her attractive bouquet of asters.

*   *   *

Inside the reception, the guests were also buzzing around, already attacking the drink station. Mom was on top of it already though, so I went to prepare cake #1. I had carefully rehearsed my balancing act, so I was handling it all okay, if not gracefully. I was in a groove: cut a row, cut some columns, slap on a sugar daisy. Repeat.

As I happened to glance up from my work, I noticed something moving on the side wall a few feet away. Upon closer examination, I saw eight or ten ants merrily marching around to nowhere in particular. *Oh no, please not that!* I thought. I immediately checked around the kitchen to make sure no insect armies had approached the food area. They had not, and seemed to show no interest in doing so. Either these ants were lost, lazy, or stupid, but they never organized sufficiently to invade. All of the food was safe. Each cake enjoyed a successful takeoff, smooth journey across the room, and soft landing.

The reception moved along, and guests filed through the buffet line, creating an interesting serpentine obstacle course for those of us working the food and beverage line. They were a thirsty lot, too. Senator and I were now on refill detail full time. Once the tea was replenished, the water was low. Once the water was topped off, the punch was running on 'e'.

It was on one of these punch runs that I finally got to cool off. Despite the air conditioning, I had been sweating and hoping that I did not smell too repulsive, or at least that Senator would give me a head's up if I did. As I quickly removed the lid of the punch server, I was very suddenly reminded that it stored ice in a top compartment, which kept it from diluting the drink. The ice, which by this time was icy water, drained thoroughly down the front of my dress, soaking me in the process. Nobody noticed except Jackie, who ran for a mop. *Well, that about figures.* I dabbed at my dripping chest, glad that I wasn't the one wearing white.

Once the guests had eaten, the toasts had been made, the new couple had danced, and the bridal cake had been officially cut, things finally slowed down a little. I plopped down next to my grandma, noticing my name on a placecard. It was the first time I had made it over to the table. Senator still hadn't sat down. Out of the corner of my eye I noticed him bringing Caleb food as he continued to man the d.j. operations. My aunt teased my grandma, telling her she should try to catch the bridal bouquet that was about to be thrown. "Aw get outta' here!" Grandma joked in return. "At my age, all men want is a nurse or a purse!"

The party died down and eventually ended. My sister came up to me, still beaming, and thanked me for our work. At that point, I really had no idea how things had appeared to her; I just hoped that it didn't seem too stressful or chaotic. I hoped she had a great time. "I think I got some good pictures..." I blurted out, knowing what a photobug she is.

"Thank you! You know how much I love pictures!" (See, what did I tell you?) "I'm so excited! Everything was just how we wanted it!" Really? This from a recent sting victim whose veil nearly flew off of her head due to the intense breeze? I was both surprised and relieved. Then it occurred to me that, from her perspective, the wedding probably was perfect. Her friends and family had just witnessed her marry a guy whom she absolutely adored, and who adored her in return. Who needed cold running water?

Heidi hugged me and ran off with her groom. Senator and I nibbled some olives and cheese cubes before starting the process of packing up. I looked around the room at the post-party mess, which all things considered, was not that bad. A bridesmaid and another friend of Heidi's started gathering centerpieces. My mom wondered aloud what she was going to do with an extra eighty (still ant-free!) pieces of cake. My brothers started to dismantle sound gear. Outside, my dad went out to clear space in his now-drivable van. All of us would have to work quickly and efficiently in one last push, for just then the thunder and lightning began.

Afterword

Why do I insist on visiting all of these places and experiencing them in person? Because a picture is *only* worth 1,000 words. (That's not nearly enough for a book.) Perhaps the opportunity or even desire to travel will not always be part of me. I doubt it, but if that happens, I will turn to photographs, travelogues, and documentaries. In the meantime, I will turn my wheels. Travel is evolution, and I hope to be a better person for it.

~Wendy V
May 2013

The Pewter Candlestick
(inspired by Jean Bonnet Tavern,
The Body Snatcher, & *Adelé*)

Carnaby Meriston Hackworth did not hate me. I tried to convince myself once again. Or more precisely, Lieutenant Hackworth was not capable of hating me or anyone else in that mono-dimensional ilk typical of a military man who had seen thirty-two years in the North Country. No, he was far too gallant, too deferential, and, as more than one soul would attest, too evil. Hate me he did not.

I picked up his letter of the fifth and reclined in my chair, re-reading his invitation yet again in the quickly dimming light. The oaken seat creaked, complaining of its broken rail. I addressed my chair directly, if pointlessly: *When I have secured my fortune, you shall be repaired, draped in velvet, and then cast out into the street for the beggars to spit upon. Stupid Stool*, I thought to myself, shifting my weight to ease its burden. I rubbed my eyes and picked up my quill to respond.

It is with great hon— I stopped before completing the word. How could anyone accept any proposal of Hackworth's with anything resembling honor? For the past fortnight I had questioned incessantly my own sanity in even the temptation of entering a business arrangement with such a man.

On the other hand, what was honor to a man who had just spent his last shilling on a pint of poorly poured ale? To enhance my misery, it was served by such a wretched barmaid as should be paid *not* to go to bed with. Horrors-- I can still picture the deep black caverns where her sparse yellow teeth once had more companions. I breathed deeply and began again.

I humbly accept your generous offer as indicated in your letter of the 5th. Humbly indeed. Twilight was rapidly waning. I searched my purse for a flint with which to light the candle on the desk, finding a small but useful chip. Pride had slipped from my vain clutches long before coming to such mean circumstances.

Asea, we were told that a man's worth was measured by the number of stars under which he sailed. I had always questioned such tallying however, arguing that those of us who sailed under tumultuous skies rarely saw stars, yet weren't we the braver? Or maybe the stars were the problem, though Adelé had never thought so. She would laugh off even the most pressing matters, reducing all such instances to trivial, childlike games. But Adelé is long gone, and a man well into his third score of years has no business with children or their games. Lieutenant Hackworth would certainly play no games upon our meeting next month, yet he might still manage a way to cheat.

I picked up my quill to continue. *I shall make all necessary preparations to meet your carriage at sunset on the 31st. You may depend upon my utmost confidentiality. It is my great hope that we might meet some common understanding, satisfactory to both of our estates. Until such time, I remain*

Yours faithfully,

I dipped my quill into the ink once more before signing. When the ink had dried sufficiently, I folded the note, somewhat surprised by the steadiness of my hands. The deed was now set in motion. From the drawer I took my father's seal. I tipped the candle slightly, permitting a few splashes of wax to coat the edge of the flap. A crisply outlined Z was pressed into the solidifying liquid, testifying that the words contained within were solely mine.

* * *

Lieutenant Hackworth may not have hated me, but I am quite sure he distrusted me, as I him. Nevertheless, as the evening bells rang out, his coach appeared outside the rooms I had temporarily taken. The coachman said not a word, but stared vacantly into the street. The footman showed himself a bit more cordial. "Eve-nin' Suh. I am to bring you to Th' Dog tonight, if you please, Suh," he extended, using the local slang for The Red Dog Tavern. I did not bother to answer the man, but stepped into the cab, hoisting my cloak to clear the wheel. Once situated, I felt for the revolver at my side. Suddenly a sinking feeling came over me as I wondered why the proprietors of the public house had chosen red as their signature color.

Upon arrival at the tavern, the footman unlatched my door to reveal my prompt host. The years had not altered him, except perhaps to make him more fully... him. His frame, though not larger than an average man's, was nonetheless imposing. His thin and graying hair brushed his shoulders, doing its best to escape his menacing countenance. A wide smile spread across his dry lips. "Welcome, Friend!" He interrupted my concentrated gaze with an outstretched hand. *Oh yes, I had forgotten.* Lieutenant Hackworth was the only man I had ever known who offered his left hand in greeting. Not wanting to appear caught unguarded in even this strange gesture, I offered him my own left hand, trying to hide the natural awkwardness it entailed. This, I had determined, would set the tone of the evening's business meeting. Hackworth would lay the traps, and I would spring them and bound away. Perhaps I could play this game after all, at even my age, although I do not believe Adelé would have approved.

My host appeared taller as I stepped closer to follow him. His distinct scent of tobacco and maple permeated the air. I coughed quietly into my handkerchief. "Tonight we meet, but first we meat!" he barked, following his own pun with uproarious laughter. I smiled weakly. If all other objectives failed, I would at least have the pleasure of indulging in the tavern's famed victuals.

We climbed the three crooked stone steps to the heavy wooden door. Before Hackworth could pound out our arrival, a rather pretty maid opened it before us, bowing longer and deeper than necessary. "I see we have right gentlemen dining with us," she announced, apparently speaking to the ground.

I offered my hand, and, I must admit, my eyes, as I led her back up to her feet. Such a figure was not common among the washerwomen where I had lately lodged. *Would that I could exchange my dining partner for this lovely creature!* My foolish lack of prudence in revealing my interest in the angelic Sarah was Hackworth's cue to act. He immediately intervened by grabbing her free hand and pressing a sovereign into it. Her gray eyes and easily-purchased devotion toward him grew as she quickly forgot my humble attentions.

The young woman-- for she had already become nameless to me-- led us through the crowded room toward a table in the rear corner. Whether it was the chill of the night air, or the sting of rejection, I was grateful to be seated next to the crackling fire. As congenial as the young woman had been, The Red Dog provided the same scene as a hundred such establishments. Long, rough-hewn wooden beams spanned the length of the ceiling, supporting the chambers above, while fitted stone walls contained the hungry patrons within. Beneath the dusty floor, no doubt, lay kegs of brewed specialties and native roots and gourds. Somewhere in another room an oyster stew simmered, while loaves of crusty bread baked on the hearth.

"I suppose you'll raise a glass with me?" asked Hackworth.

"To what or whom?" I ventured.

"To we! To us! To our partnership's success!" Hackworth was already spilling ale in his enthusiastic toast. I gingerly complied, glass in midair. He must have noticed my reticence or read my mind-- more possible than one might suppose-- or both, because he concluded his long gulp more pensively. "You don't think I hate you, do you Matty?" No one had called me that since I was a child, and I was no more fond of it now than I was then.

"I think I'd like another pint before we discuss the details," I announced coolly.

"That's my lad, Matty! Somebody get this poor parched soul a bit of relief!" The young woman hastened to serve me, still visibly loyal to her new-found patron.

The young couple at the next table looked disapprovingly at my loud companion, but I did not bother to apologize on his behalf. For now they could forgive anyone simply by looking into each other's eyes. Soon enough they would know their own noisy skirmishes. I sipped my broth, which had lately arrived, as I wondered how and when to breach the subject for which we had found ourselves in this peculiar camaraderie. After all, procrastination was solving nothing but my hunger pangs.

"Lieutenant Hackworth, as I understand it, you would be willing to supply me with the approximate sum of two thousand pounds. Is that correct?" I began.

"Two thousand? Why not five thousand? Why not ten? Do you really think your trivial amount means any more to me than as many damned beans?"

"Then why not simply give me the money, as a sort of gift for the sake of our past?" I was feeling bolder now, due in part, I am sure, to the spirits.

"Oh Matty. Matty. My forlorn mourning Matty..." he trailed off, quoting a line from an obscure nursery rhyme.

(Hackworth fancied himself an expert in all things literary, provided they were composed for audiences of no more than six years old.) "I care not about money, justly obtained or otherwise. It is the sport of the thing, my money mourning Matty! What, I ask, what joy would I derive from a stoic visit with your creditors? I'd grace their doorsteps, pay your debt, sip a likely ill-steeped tea, bid them a good afternoon, and be on my most dull way…"

He continued his rant, but I ignored his diatribe, saving what was left of my dwindling attention span for the part where he would explain my end of the bargain. Instead, I turned my interest to the conversations around me. A group of sailors at a nearby table traded stories of recent travels. It seemed a ship bound for Portugal had left port this morning, only to turn back under mutinous attack. How I longed for my seafaring days, now more than ever.

"…Which comes to your assignment, Matty. Are you familiar with a village, about twelve miles from here, commonly called Garristown?…" At another table, two old friends shared a pork pie while reminiscing about their youth. John (as I had overheard his name) was once chased for over an hour by a minister's angry wife, whose wash he had ruined with his invented game of pitching cranberries. Wills, in turn, relayed the tale of his mischievous brother, who took the wicked opportunity to steal his clothes while he swam one afternoon. It seemed a well-placed bundle of leaves had served him as well as it did Adam.

"You'll know him by his distinct feature. One of his ears is nipped near the lobe…" I managed a smile as Sarah delivered a plate of warm bread and a cup of cream. I could not place blame on a girl who was only trying to make her way as I was—both of us using Lieutenant Hackworth to meet our needs. He did not hate Sarah, either.

When she left to wait on others, I noticed one more patron, whom I had previously missed in my survey of the room. This woman was old and alone, surely an unusual site in any tavern, yet she looked quite at home at The Red Dog. Quietly she nibbled her bread, until she discovered my curious glance. At once, she raised her glass to me. Perhaps someone had once tossed cranberries into her washing, too. *Anyone—why can't I be here with anyone else tonight? Anyone but him!*

"And when you have satisfactorily completed the task, Matty, you shall be justly rewarded. My coach will meet you outside the blacksmith shop, and you will get in as though you had not a care in the world. My coachman will convey you unto me, and I will give you further instruction at that time. Is it agreed then?" He waited several seconds for my reply. It was the first time all evening that my host had been silent. I shivered. The fire was dying out, and no one was bothering to rekindle it.

"It is agreed," I answered, not fully knowing or caring about the details to which I had just committed myself. Hackworth beamed, clearly approving of our arrangement. He paid for our meal, pressing another sovereign into Sarah's free palm, and pressing Sarah with his free hand.

The rogue. I couldn't stand to see or hear anymore. Feeling no obligation to wait for my host, I hurried to the door, desperate for fresh air. Before I could make my escape, I was stopped by a gentleman. I had forgotten that he had taken my cloak when we first arrived. He helped me slip it around my shoulders before I entered the damp fog of the night.

I thanked him and he replied, "Glad to have you, Sir, especially on a night like this. Why, if it wasn't for you, we'd have had not a single guest." Somewhere, in the other room, I heard Sarah giggle.

www.ingramcontent.com/pod-product-compliance
Lightning Source LLC
LaVergne TN
LVHW041631070426
835507LV00008B/568